THE COMMON LAW LIBRA

[redacted]

CHARLESWORTH & PERCY ON NEGLIGENCE

VOLUMES IN THE COMMON LAW LIBRARY

Arlidge, Eady & Smith on Contempt
Benjamin's Sale of Goods
Bowstead & Reynolds on Agency
Bullen & Leake & Jacob's Precedents of Pleadings
Charlesworth & Percy on Negligence
Chitty on Contracts
Clerk & Lindsell on Torts
Gatley on Libel and Slander
Goff & Jones on Unjust Enrichment
Jackson & Powell on Professional Liability
McGregor on Damages
Phipson on Evidence

THE COMMON LAW LIBRARY

CHARLESWORTH & PERCY ON NEGLIGENCE

FIRST SUPPLEMENT TO THE FIFTEENTH EDITION

Up to date to 10 February 2023

MARK ARMITAGE, MA (CANTAB) LLM (CANTAB)
A Barrister of Crown Office Chambers, Inner Temple

RICHARD HYDE, PHD
Professor of Law, Regulation and Governance, University of Nottingham

PETER MORTON LLB, LLM (CANTAB)
A Barrister of Crown Office Chambers, Inner Temple

SWEET & MAXWELL

THOMSON REUTERS

Published in 2023 by Thomson Reuters, trading as Sweet & Maxwell.
Thomson Reuters is registered in England & Wales, Company No.1679046.
Registered Office and address for service:
5 Canada Square, Canary Wharf, London, E14 5AQ.

For further information on our products and services, visit *http://www.sweetandmaxwell.co.uk*.

Computerset by Sweet & Maxwell.
Printed and bound by CPI Group (UK) Ltd, Croydon, CR0 4YY.
A CIP catalogue record of this book is available from the British Library.

ISBN (First Supplement print): 978-0-414-11252-0

ISBN (First Supplement e-book): 978-0-414-11254-4

ISBN (First Supplement print and e-book): 978-0-414-11253-7

For orders and enquiries, go to: *http://www.tr.com/uki-legal-contact*; Tel: 0345 600 9355.

HH JUDGE WALTON (1949 TO 2023)

I am saddened to report the recent death of HH Judge Christopher Walton who passed away on 9 April 2023 at the age of just 74.

Having read law at Downing College, Cambridge, Christopher was called to the bar in 1973 and practised with distinction from Broad Chare Chambers in Newcastle. He was a Recorder from 1992 until 1997 and then became the Designated Civil Judge at Newcastle.

A highly regarded civil practitioner, Christopher became involved in *Charlesworth & Percy* when he worked with Rodney Percy on the Ninth Edition in 1997. He then took over the reins for the following five editions until his retirement in 2021. His diligence, care and meticulous eye for detail saw the book flourish under his stewardship. The scale of his contribution to this work cannot be overstated. I will personally be ever grateful for the time he took in mentoring me; always willing to cast an eye over my work and ready at hand with helpful suggestions.

Christopher will be greatly missed by all members of the *Charlesworth & Percy* editorial team and all those with whom he worked at Sweet & Maxwell, and in particular Sohini Banerjee, senior publisher at Thomson Reuters, with whom he worked for many years.

Our thoughts are with his family at this very sad time.

Mark Armitage
5 May 2023

HOW TO USE THIS SUPPLEMENT

This is the First Supplement to the Fifteenth Edition of *Charlesworth & Percy on Negligence* and has been compiled according to the structure of the main work.

At the beginning of each chapter of this Supplement, a mini table of contents has been included. Where a heading in this table of contents has been marked with a square pointer (■), this indicates that there is relevant information in this Supplement to which the reader should refer. Within each chapter, updating information is referenced to the relevant paragraph in the main work.

PREFACE

The legal world has moved at pace over the last year. Claims have increasingly been heard inside courtrooms rather than on virtual platforms; and the Court Service should be commended for their diligence in setting about dealing with any backlog of work resulting from the restrictions of the COVID pandemic.

The High Court and Court of Appeal have added to our understanding of the newly formulated approach to the fundamental ingredients of negligence as proposed in *Manchester Building Society v Grant Thornton UK LLP* and *Khan v Meadows* and readers can now better appreciate how that approach may be applied in practice.

I am grateful to Richard Hyde who has, amongst many other matters, dealt with some interesting issues in relation to the application of *Caparo* and the duty formulae in general; the difficult questions that arise when considering the existence of a common law duty owed by a local authority exercising statutory powers; the development of the concepts underpinning the defence of illegality; and the evolution of the principles of vicarious liability.

I must also thank Peter Morton who has taken on occupiers' liability, employers' liability, breach of statutory duty and professional negligence. He has, amongst numerous other topics, considered the broad implications of the Building Safety Act 2022; the continued impact and practical consequences of s.69 of the Enterprise and Regulatory Reform Act 2013; and the application of the *Bolam* test to the sale of an 18th Century French Rococo painting.

The law is stated as at 10 February 2023.

Mark Armitage
Seaham
County Durham
5 April 2023

TABLE OF CONTENTS

TABLE OF ABBREVIATIONS

A. & E.	Adolphus & Ellis's Reports, Q.B., 1834–40
A. & S.L.	Air and Space Law
A.C	Law Reports, Appeal Cases, 1875–90
[1891] A.C.	Law Reports, Appeal Cases, 1891–
ACOP	Approved Code of Practice
AHA	Area health authority
AIDS	acquired immune deficiency syndrome
A.L.J.R.	Australian Law Journal Reports
All E.R.	All England Reports
A.L.R.	Australian Law Reports, 1834–40
App.Cas.	Law Reports, Appeal Cases (1891 onwards)
ASHE	Annual Survey of Hours and Earnings
B. & S.	Best and Smith's Reports, Q.B. 1861–70
BC	Borough Council
Bing. N.C.	Bingham's New Cases, C.P. 1834–40
BRB	British Railways Board
Brownl.	Brownlow & Goldesborough's Common Pleas Reports
BTC	British Transport Commission
B.W.C.C.	Butterworths Workmen's Compensation Reports
Cab. & El.	Cababe & Ellis' Queen's Bench Reports
C.B.	Common Bench Reports, 1840–56
CC	County Council
CD	Core duties
CHAPS	Clearing house automated payment system
[1891] Ch.	Law Reports, Chancery
Ch.D.	Law Reports, Chancery Division, 1876–90
CICA	Criminal Injuries Compensation Authority
CICB	Criminal Injuries Compensation Board
CIM	Uniform Rules Concerning the Contract of International Carriage of Goods by Rail

CIV	Uniform Rules Concerning the Contract of International Carriage of Passengers by Rail
CJEU	Court of Justice of the European Union
Cl. & F.	Clark and Finelly's Reports, HL, 1831–46
C.L.C.	Current Law Consolidation
C.L.J.	Cambridge Law Journal
C.L.Y.	Current Law Year Book
C.M.L.R.	Common Market Law Reports
Com. Cas.	Commercial Cases
Conv.	Conveyancer and Property Lawyer
COTIF	Convention concerning International Carriage by Rail
C.P.D.	Law Reports, Common Pleas Division, 1875–80
CPR	Civil Procedure Rules
CRA	Consumer Rights Act 2015
Crim. L.R.	Criminal Law Review
Cro. Eliz.	Croke's King's Bench Reports
CRU	Compensation Recovery Unit
dB	decibel
DC	District council
D.L.R.	Dominion Law Reports
DSM-V	*American Diagnostic and Statistical Manual of Mental Disorders*
Dunlop	Dunlop's Reports, Session Cases
DVT	deep vein thrombosis
DWP	Department for Work and Pensions
E. & E.	Ellis & Ellis, Q.B. Reports
Ed. C.R.	Education Case Reports
E.G.	Estates Gazette
EWCA Civ	Court of Appeal, England and Wales
EWHC	High Court, England and Wales
Ex.	Exchequer Reports, 1848–56
F. & C.L.	Finance and Credit Law
FCA	Financial Conduct Authority
F.C.R.	Family Court Reports
FSA	Financial Services Authority
FSO	Financial Services Ombudsman

H. & C.	Hurlstone and Coltman's Exch. Reports, 1862–66
H. & N.	Hurlstone and Norman's Exch. Reports, 1856–62
HA	Health Authority
ICOBS	Insurance: Conduct of Business Sourcebook
I.C.R.	Industrial Cases Reports
I.F.L. Rev.	International Financial Law Review
IH	Inner House, Court of Session
J.P.I. Law	Journal of Personal Injury Law
[1901] K.B.	Law Reports, King's Bench (1901 onwards)
K.I.R.	Knight's Industrial Law Reports
LBC	London Borough Council
Ld.Raym.	Lord Raymond's Reports, 1694–1732
L.J.Ch.	Law Journal Chancery (1831–1946)
L.J.C.P.	Law Journal Common Pleas, 1831–75
L.J.Ex.	Law Journal Reports, Exchequer (1831–75)
L.J.K.B.	Law Journal, King's Bench
L.J.Q.B.	Law Journal, Queen's Bench
Lloyd's Rep.	Lloyd's Law Reports
L.Q.R.	Law Quarterly Review
L.R.Ir.	Law Reports, Ireland, 1867–93
L.S.Gaz.	Law Society's Gazette
L.T.	Law Times Reports, 1859–1947
M. & W.	Meeson and Welsby's Exchequer Reports, 1836–47
Macq.	Macqueen's Reports, Session Cases
MBC	Metropolitan health authority
M.C.L.Q.	Lloyd's Maritime and Commercial Law Quarterly
MIB	Motor Insurers' Bureau
M.L.R.	Modern Law Review
NCB	National Coal Board
NERC	National Environment Research Council
NHS	National Health Service
N.I.	Northern Irish Reports

NICE	National Institute for Health and Care Excellence
N.L.J.	New Law Journal
New L.J.	[also used]
N.Z.L.R.	New Zealand Law Reports
OH	Outer House, Court of Session
O.J.L.S.	Oxford Journal of Legal Studies
PCC	Professional Consultancy Certificate
PD	Practice Direction
Phillips	Phillips' Chancery Reports
P.I.Q.R.	Personal Injury and Quantum Reports
P.N.	Professional Negligence Reports
P.N.L.R.	Professional Negligence and Liability Reports
PTSD	post-traumatic stress disorder
Q.B.	Law Reports, Queen's Bench, 1865–75
[1891] Q.B.	Law Reports, Queen's Bench (1891 onwards)
Q.B.D.	Law Reports, Queen's Bench Division
Q.L.R.	Queensland Law Reports
RSA	Returned Services Association
RSC	Rules of the Supreme Court
R.T.R.	Road Traffic Reports
S.A.	South African Law Reports
S.A.S.R.	South Australian State Reports
S.C.	Session Cases
S.C.L.R.	Scottish Civil Law Reports
SHA	Strategic Health Authority
S.J.	Solicitor's Journal
S.L.T.	Scots Law Times
SRA	Solicitors Regulation Authority
SRN	state registered nurse
T.L.R.	Times Law Reports, 1885–1952
Tort L. Rev.	Tort Law Review
UCTA	Unfair Contract Terms Act 1977
UKHL	House of Lords, United Kingdom
W.A.L.R.	Western Australian Law Reports
W.L.R.	Weekly Law Reports
W.N.	Weekly Notes, 1866–1952

W.W.R.	Western Weekly Reports

TABLE OF CASES

TABLE OF STATUTES

TABLE OF STATUTORY INSTRUMENTS

TABLE OF CIVIL PROCEDURE RULES

Chapter 1

THE MEANING OF NEGLIGENCE

Table of Contents

3. Negligence as the Breach of a Duty to Take Care

The modern law of negligence reformulated

Replace paragraph 1-47 with:

Subsequent to the decisions in *Khan v Meadows* and *Manchester Building Society*, the Court of Appeal in *Spire Property Development LLP v Withers LLP*[108a] has indeed emphasised the importance of the newly formulated approach particularly when dealing with issues involving the scope of an alleged duty of care and how that question is to be addressed in the context of the law of negligence in general. There was no suggestion that the new formulation, as a general rule, was designed to supplant the traditional tripartite approach to negligence actions, rather that it is a very useful mechanism of analysing those cases where issues pertaining to the scope of the duty of care may be of paramount importance: 1-47

> "The decisions in *Manchester* and *Khan* addressed the concept of scope of duty in the tort of negligence as illustrated by the decision of the House of Lords in *Banque Bruxelles Lambert SA v Eagle Star Insurance Co Ltd; South Australia Asset Management Corpn v York Montague Ltd* [1997] AC 191 ("*SAAMCO*"). The majority opinion was set out in the speech of Lords Hodge and Sales. The majority suggested a six-stage analysis as a useful (though non-prescriptive) approach to placing the scope of duty principle in the tort of negligence: see *Manchester* at [6]; *Khan* at [28]. The second question asked what were the risks of harm to the claimant against which the law imposes on the defendant a duty to take care. It held (at [4]) that the scope of that duty was "governed by the purpose of the duty, judged on an objective basis by reference to the purpose for which the advice is being given" ("the purpose test") and at [17] that "in the case of negligent advice given by a professional adviser one looks to see what risk the duty was supposed to guard against and then looks to see whether the loss suffered represented the fruition of that risk."[108b]

[108a] *Spire Property Development LLP v Withers LLP* [2022] EWCA Civ 970; [2022] P.N.L.R. 27.

[108b] *Spire Property Development LLP v Withers LLP* [2022] EWCA Civ 970 at [70], per Carr LJ.

After paragraph 1-47, add new paragraphs:

This opinion in relation to the relevance of the newly formulated approach is echoed in the judgment of Richards J in *Aurium Real Estate London Ultra Prime Ltd v Mishcon De Reya LLP*,[108c] who considered that: 1-48

> "In *Manchester Building Society v Grant Thornton LLP* [2021] UKSC 20 and *Meadows v Khan* [2021] UKSC 21, the Supreme Court gave general guidance regarding the proper approach to determining the scope of duty and the extent of liability of professional advisers in the tort of negligence."

108c *Aurium Real Estate London Ultra Prime Ltd v Mishcon De Reya LLP* [2022] EWHC 1253 (Ch).

1-49 The Court of Appeal in *Armstead v Royal Sun Alliance Insurance Co Ltd*,[108d] considered the six questions set out in *Manchester* and *Khan*, but more as a "cross check"[108e] in relation to liability and once a substantive determination had been made on existing authority.

108d *Armstead v Royal Sun Alliance Insurance Co Ltd* [2022] EWCA Civ 497; [2022] R.T.R. 23 (which considers the extent to which a negligent party is liable in bailment for damage to hired equipment).

108e *Armstead v Royal Sun Alliance Insurance Co Ltd* [2022] EWCA Civ 497 at [58], per Dingemans LJ.

1-50 The new test has also been applied when considering the extent of the duty of care owed by a single joint expert instructed in tribunal proceedings.[108f] Again, it was the scope of duty question that presented the most difficult aspect of the case and the expert's duty of care was held not to extend to protecting the claimant from the risk of an adverse credibility finding, or a finding of dishonesty.

108f *Radia v Marks* [2022] EWHC 145 (QB); [2022] P.N.L.R. 12, see also Ch.3, para.3-20.

1-51 In another case, had it been necessary, the newly formulated approach would have been adopted to deny liability for the alleged negligence of several midwives who were said to have failed to administer a sufficient quantity of a labour inducing drug, resulting in the claimant being born with cerebral palsy.[108g] Albeit an *obiter dictum*, given that there was no breach of duty on the part of the midwives, Lady Wise set out the newly formulated approach, and found that the loss would have been too remote and that there was insufficient nexus between the alleged breach of duty and the harm sustained.[108h]

108g *D v Grampian Health Board* [2022] CSOH 63.

108h *D v Grampian Health Board* [2022] CSOH 63 at [174], per Lady Wise. This was perhaps unsurprising given that there was no evidence that there would have been a different outcome had the midwives administered additional amounts of the drug; the case would undoubtedly have failed due to a lack of causation without any need to refer to the newly formulated approach.

CHAPTER 2

THE DUTY TO TAKE CARE

TABLE OF CONTENTS

1. CONCEPT OF A DUTY OF CARE

(B) Duty formulae

Application of Robinson

After paragraph 2-23, add new paragraph:

2-23a The Judicial Committee of the Privy Council considered the incremental development of the law in *Royal Bank of Scotland International Ltd v JP SPC 4*.[54a] The board noted that the "incrementalism and the reliance in *Caparo v Dickman* on what is fair, just and reasonable go together" because "one needs to resort to underlying judgement as to what is fair, just and reasonable" in order to "explain which are the factors that are relevant for an analogy to be drawn" between an existing duty of care and a novel case.[54b] In *JP SPC 4*, the Privy Council refused to reason by analogy and extend the *Quincecare*[54c] duty to a third party with whom the bank had no contractual relationship, as it would "not be fair, just and reasonable to impose a duty of care [in this case]. This would place an unacceptable burden on banks going outside their contractual relationship with their customers."[54d]

[54a] *Royal Bank of Scotland International Ltd v JP SPC 4* [2022] UKPC 18; [2022] 3 W.L.R. 261, see also para.2-54.

[54b] *JP SPC 4* [2022] UKPC 18 at [80].

[54c] *Barclays Bank Plc v Quincecare Ltd* [1992] 4 All E.R. 363 QBD (Comm), see further Ch.10, para.10-100 and Ch.4, para.4-272.

[54d] *JP SPC 4* [2022] UKPC 18, see also para.2-54.

Scope of the duty

After "outside its scope.", add new footnote 68a:

[68a] For example, in *Wokingham BC v Arshad* [2022] EWHC 2419 (KB); [2023] R.T.R. 9, psychiatric harm suffered as a consequence of negligent advice on a licensing matter provided by a local authority was held to be outside the scope of the duty, whereas pure economic loss would have fallen within the scope. See also para.2-288a. **2-27**

(C) Application of the Caparo analysis

(iii) Fair, just and reasonable

Protecting the vulnerable

Replace paragraph 2-51 with:

One important policy consideration can be whether, or the extent to which, a claimant comes within a category of persons which can be seen as deserving of legal protection. The principle has both a positive and a negative aspect. There is a concern to protect those at a disadvantage, who have no reasonably available means of protecting themselves.[121] Decisions recognising a duty of care owed by a surveyor to the purchaser of a defective house,[122] and by a solicitor to the disappointed legatees of a will that the solicitor had failed to execute,[123] are examples. On the other hand, if a person is well positioned to look after him or herself, a duty may be thought to be unnecessary or inappropriate. The focus is on the steps a person reasonably could have taken to look after his or her own interests. So, accountants reporting on the state of a company's accounts were under no duty to prospective purchasers of the company, who it would be anticipated would consult with their own accountancy advisers.[124] And no duty was owed to buyers of goods that were damaged by the defendants when in transit and at a time before the buyers became the owners, partly because the buyers could have protected their interests in their contract with the sellers.[125] It was not necessary to impose a duty of care on a university to take reasonable care for the wellbeing, health and safety of a disabled student, because the student was afforded protection by the Equality Act 2010.[125a] **2-51**

[121] See generally Todd, "Personal liability, vicarious liability, non-delegable duties and protecting vulnerable people" (2016) 23 Tort L.J. 105.

[122] *Smith v Eric S Bush* [1990] 1 A.C. 831; see para.2-237.

[123] *White v Jones* [1995] 2 A.C. 207; see para.2-267.

[124] *James McNaughton Paper Group Ltd v Hicks Anderson & Co* [1991] 2 Q.B. 113; see para.2-240; *Esanda Finance Corp Ltd v Peat Marwick Hungerfords* (1997) 188 C.L.R. 241, 284 HCA.

[125] *Leigh and Sillavan Ltd v Aliakmon Shipping Co Ltd: The Aliakmon* [1986] A.C. 785; see para.2-257.

[125a] *Abrahart v University of Bristol* [2022] P.I.Q.R. P17 CC (Bristol).

Maintaining coherence in the legal system

Replace paragraph 2-54 with:

A similar principle applies where the question is whether a duty of care in negligence can co-exist with other rules of the common law. Expanding negligence liability into novel areas might tend to disrupt the policy balance struck by existing rules of tort which impose a stricter form of liability. For example, an action **2-54** for negligence in bringing a criminal prosecution against a claimant has been rejected in circumstances where an action for malicious prosecution would lie.[128] In a different context, the argument that a duty of care would undermine the principle of privity of contract, while emphatically rejected in *Donoghue v Stevenson*,[129] carries greater weight in cases where loss is purely financial. This is a continuing source of tension in misstatement cases, where claimants sue in respect of negligent words without having given any contractual consideration in return. It has been called the "free rider" argument.[130] Another possibility is the impact of a duty on core principles of constitutional law. A distinction in public body cases between "policy" matters and "operational" matters is founded ultimately on the need for a proper separation of powers between courts and public bodies exercising discretionary functions. So a duty is owed only in respect of operational or "justiciable" matters, where the policy-making functions of the public body are not called in question.[131] Similarly, it was not necessary to impose a duty of care on a university to take reasonable care for the wellbeing, health and safety of a disabled student, because the student was afforded protection by the Equality Act 2010.[131a] Further, in *Royal Bank of Scotland International Ltd v JP SPC 4*,[131b] the Privy Council held that a bank did not owe a duty to non-customers in respect of fraudulent activity by which money beneficially owned by the claimant was paid out of accounts held with the bank by a company. Such a duty would "place an unacceptable burden on banks going outside their contractual relationship with their customers"[131c] and would not add coherence to the legal system.

[128] See e.g. *Calveley v Chief Constable of Merseyside Police* [1989] A.C. 1228, 1238; see para.2-380.

[129] *Donoghue v Stevenson* [1932] A.C. 562.

[130] e.g. *Caparo Industries Plc v Dickman* [1990] 2 A.C. 605; see paras 2-221 to 2-223.

[131] e.g. *Barrett v Enfield LBC* [2001] 2 A.C. 550; see para.2-354.

[131a] *Abrahart v University of Bristol* [2022] P.I.Q.R. P17, see also para.2-51.

[131b] *Royal Bank of Scotland International Ltd v JP SPC 4* [2022] UKPC 18, see also para.2-23a.

[131c] *Royal Bank of Scotland International Ltd v JP SPC 4* [2022] UKPC 18 at [80].

2. THE KIND OF CONDUCT

(B) Omissions

(iv) Assuming responsibility for other persons

Responsibility for another's welfare

Replace footnote 213 with:

2-89 [213] Parents: *McCallion v Dodd* [1966] N.Z.L.R. 710 CA; *Tweed Shire Council v Howarth* (2009) Aus Torts Reps 82-010, NSWCA; Local authority: *Barrett v Enfield LBC* [1999] 3 W.L.R. 79 HL. School: *Barnes v Hants CC* [1969] 1 W.L.R. 1563 HL; *Commonwealth v Introvigne* (1982) 150 C.L.R. 258 HCA; *Myers v Peel County Board of Education* [1981] 2 S.C.R. 21 SCC. Whether or how far a duty of this kind might extend to cover the promotion by parents of a child's general well-being was considered by the New Zealand Court of Appeal in *A v Roman Catholic Archdiocese of Wellington* [2008] 3 N.Z.L.R. 289. William Young P explained that a claim for bad parenting would not be entertained, for reasons of parental autonomy and justiciability. But there could be a duty as to children's physical and psychiatric health and this would encompass emotional abuse. In *OPO v MLA* [2014] EWCA Civ 1277 at [57], the court rejected a claim alleging a parent owed a duty to a child not to expose him to unacceptable risk of psychological injury. Arden LJ said that it would encompass a whole range of commonplace activities in which a parent was involved in caring for his child. On appeal to the Supreme

Court in *Rhodes v OPO* [2015] UKSC 32; [2016] A.C. 219 the Court of Appeal's finding that there could nonetheless be a claim under the rule in *Wilkinson v Downton* on the facts in this case was reversed. On the obligation of schools to protect children against bullying, see Elvin, "The duty of schools to prevent bullying" (2003) 11 Tort L.R. 168; English, "Liability for bullying: holding schools accountable" (2011) 19 Tort L.R. 41. See also *Ellis v Kelly* [2018] EWHC 2031 (QB); [2018] 4 W.L.R. 124 (it was undesirable to impose a duty of care to regulate decisions and actions arising in the course of normal daily parenting). A similar duty does not arise in relation to university students, see *Abrahart v University of Bristol* [2022] P.I.Q.R. P17 County Court (Bristol). See also para.2-51.

(v) Assuming responsibility by taking on a task

Assuming responsibility to perform professional services

After "to the claimants.", add new footnote 274a:

[274a] The extent of the assumption of responsibility is a question that must be answered in light of the facts found by the trial judge. For example, a firm of solicitors may assume responsibility for a particular task, but such a duty will not extend to matters which are not reasonably incidental to the task for which the solicitor is responsible (see *Spire Property Development LLP v Withers LLP* [2022] EWCA Civ 970; [2022] P.N.L.R. 27, where solicitors responded to three specific questions received from the claimants but did not provide advice on the remedies available. The Court of Appeal held that they had not assumed responsibility to provide advice regarding these remedies). **2-111**

3. THE KIND OF HARM

(C) Psychiatric injury

(v) Further categories of claimant

After paragraph 2-188, add new paragraph:

Advisees In *Wokingham BC v Arshad*,[460a] Bourne J held that the local authority did not owe a duty with respect to psychiatric harm suffered by the claimant in circumstances where the authority had negligently provided advice regarding the types of vehicle that would be granted a hackney carriage vehicle license. Whilst a duty may extend to pure economic loss suffered as a result of the advice, the psychiatric injury suffered by the claimant was unforeseeable. **2-188a**

[460a] *Wokingham BC v Arshad* [2022] EWHC 2419 (KB).

5. THE KIND OF DEFENDANT

(E) Public bodies

(v) Omissions to act

Generally

After "by public bodies.", add new footnote 866a:

[866a] In *FXJ v Secretary of State for the Home Department* [2022] EWHC 1531 (QB); [2023] P.I.Q.R. P1, Choudhury J considered whether the harm was caused by the action or inaction of the defendant. The claimant was subject to a deportation order made by the Secretary of State. This order was overturned by the Upper Tribunal and permission to appeal refused. Two months after the deadline for a request for permission to be made directly to the Court of Appeal, the Secretary of State filed a notice of appeal and applied for an extension of time. This caused the claimant's mental health to deteriorate, which led to 43 days of compulsory detention under mental health legislation. The notice of appeal was **2-357**

later withdrawn. Choudhury J held that although the act of making the appeal was the immediate trigger for the damage, when taken in the round this was a case concerning a failure to confer a benefit (of favourable immigration status), and therefore no duty of care was owed, as the claimant could not show that there were any applicable exceptions to the principle that a failure to confer a benefit does not generally give rise to a duty of care.

The police

After "to the criminal.", add new footnote 874a:

2-358 [874a] In *Magill v Chief Constable of the PSNI* [2022] NICA 49, the Court of Appeal refused to strike out a claim in circumstances where the claimant had been struck by a missile thrown from an Orange Order parade that had been stopped by the police. The pleadings claimed that the injuries had been caused by a combination of acts and omissions by the police which had created a danger to the public, and therefore it was arguable a duty of care could arise in this case.

Assumed responsibility

Replace footnote 886 with:

2-365 [886] See *Tindall v Chief Constable of Thames Valley* [2022] EWCA Civ 25 (no duty of care where police attended an accident and erected, then subsequently removed, a warning sign). The Court of Appeal held that the Scottish case of *Gibson v Orr* 1999 S.C. 420, which held that the police officers who failed to ensure that barriers preventing access were placed on both sides of a collapsed bridge owed a duty to road users, was contrary to the decisions in *East Suffolk Rivers Catchment Board v Kent* [1941] A.C. 74 and *Gorringe v Calderdale MBC* [2004] UKHL 15; [2004] 1 W.L.R. 1057, and did not represent the law in England and Wales. *Tindall* was applied in *CJ v Chief Constable of Wiltshire* [2022] EWHC 1661 (QB); [2023] P.I.Q.R. P2, where the careless investigation of a report that an individual, who later went on to sexually assault the claimants, was in possession of indecent images was held not to give rise to a duty of care as the failure was a mere failure to confer a benefit (which would not give rise to a duty absent control over the perpetrator or an assumption of responsibility) rather than an act. Contrast *Magill v Chief Constable of the PSNI* [2022] NICA 49, where the Court of Appeal refused to strike out a claim because it was arguable that the acts of the police had created a danger to the public which they had failed to abate, see para.2-358.

Social welfare officers

Replace footnote 908 with:

2-370 [908] *Poole BC v GN* [2019] UKSC 25; [2020] A.C. 780 at [43] and see *HXA v Surrey CC* [2022] EWCA Civ 1196; [2023] 1 W.L.R. 116 at [90]–[107]. See further para.2-372.

After paragraph 2-372, add new paragraph:

2-372a GN was applied in *HXA v Surrey CC*,[915a] where the Court of Appeal refused to strike out a claim in which it was alleged that a local authority had assumed responsibility for children by (in one case) providing respite accommodation under Children Act 1989 s.20 (with the assumption of responsibility arguably extending beyond the period of time when the child was accommodated) and (in another case) taking specific action to protect the child claimant and seeking legal advice regarding care proceedings with respect to the claimant. *HXA* casts some doubt on the correctness of the decision in *DFX v Wolverhampton CC*,[915b] suggesting that an assumption of responsibility may arise when an expert's report is obtained to assist a local authority to assess the level of risk of harm to a child in his parents' care.[915c] Whether the local authority has assumed responsibility will be a question that turns on the steps taken by the local authority, and the statutory duties and powers that underpin those actions. In *HXA*, it was held to be at least arguable that the local authority's actions were capable of amounting to an assumption of responsibility.

[915a] *HXA v Surrey CC* [2022] EWCA Civ 1196. For a commentary see Jonathan Morgan, "A riddle wrapped in an enigma: assumption of responsibility, again" (2022) 81(3) C.L.J. 449.

[915b] *DFX v Coventry City Council* [2021] EWHC 1382 (QB); [2021] P.I.Q.R. P18.

[915c] *HXA v Surrey CC* [2022] EWCA Civ 1196 at [97].

(vii) Statutory context

Other protective powers

After "court or tribunal.", add new footnote 953a:

[953a] See also *FXJ v Secretary of State for the Home Department* [2022] EWHC 1531 (QB), see para.2-357. **2-385**

(viii) Impact of European Human Rights law

Claim for causing or failing to prevent torture or inhuman or degrading treatment

After "by non-state agents.", add new footnote 986a:

[986a] The obligation under art.3 to conduct an investigation only arises once there has been a report of treatment contrary to art.3. In *CJ v Chief Constable of Wiltshire* [2022] EWHC 1661 (QB), a report regarding the possession of indecent images was held not to trigger the obligation to conduct an effective investigation under art.3. **2-408**

Limitation

Replace footnote 1008 with:

[1008] Human Rights Act 1998 s.7(5). The court extended the period under s.7(5) in *CJ v Chief Constable of Wiltshire* [2022] EWHC 1661 (QB), see para.2-408. **2-412**

Chapter 3

PARTIES

Table of Contents

1. The Crown

Acts binding on the Crown

Replace footnote 24 with:

[24] Factories Act 1961 s.173. Other relevant Acts are the Law Reform (Personal Injuries) Act 1948 s.4; the Occupiers' Liability Act 1957 s.6; the Defective Premises Act 1972 s.5; the Congenital Disabilities (Civil Liability) Act 1976 s.5; the Civil Liability (Contribution) Act 1978 s.5; the Limitation Act 1980 s.37; the Occupiers' Liability Act 1984 s.3; the Building Act 1984 (as amended by the Building Safety Act 2022) s.131A; the Latent Damage Act 1986 s.3; the Consumer Protection Act 1987 ss.1–9. **3-06**

2. JUDGES AND QUASI JUDGES, PROSECUTORS, THE POLICE

Judicial acts

Replace footnote 44 with:

3-14 [44] *Sirros v Moore* [1975] Q.B. 118. In *Magennis v Northern Ireland Courts and Tribunals Service* [2022] NIQB 6, the Clerk of Petty Sessions was held to have judicial immunity in a claim brought regarding the good faith issue of warrants beyond the jurisdiction of the Magistrates' Court.

Expert witnesses

After "been struck out.[59]", add:

3-20 A single joint expert owes a duty of care in negligence to both the claimant and defendant in a case in which they are instructed, notwithstanding the single joint expert's overarching duty to the court. However, such a duty does not extend to protecting either party from the risk of an adverse credibility finding or a finding of dishonesty.[59a]

[59a] *Radia v Marks* [2022] EWHC 145 (QB); [2022] P.N.L.R. 12.

3. THE ARMED FORCES

Peacekeeping operations

Replace footnote 82 with:

3-27 [82] *Bici v Ministry of Defence* [2004] EWHC 786 (QB). Different issues may well arise where civilians are injured in the course of armed conflict: see X. Yang, "Absolute immunity of foreign armed forces from tôrt proceedings" (2012) 71(2) C.L.J. 282, in which the author draws attention to the decision of the ICJ in *Case Concerning the Jurisdictional Immunities of the State (Germany v Italy)* [2012] ICJ Reports 99 and see the discussion of the defence of Crown Act of State above para.3-25.

5. FOREIGN SOVEREIGNS, OTHER HEADS OF STATE, AMBASSADORS, PUBLIC OFFICIALS AND VISITING ARMED FORCES

Foreign sovereign or other head of state

Replace paragraph 3-37 with:

3-37 At common law no action lies against a foreign sovereign or other head of state, unless he submits to the jurisdiction, for any tort committed personally by him.[98] As Lord Atkin stated:

> "The courts of a country will not implead a foreign sovereign, that is, they will not by their process make him against his will a party to legal proceedings whether the proceedings involve process against his person or seek to recover from him specific property or damages."[99]

Section 20 of the State Immunity Act 1978 affirmed the immunity[99a] and extended, with any necessary modification, the Diplomatic Privileges Act 1964, so as to apply its provisions to those members of a foreign head of state's family who form part of his or her household or private servants, just as its provisions apply to heads of diplomatic missions, their household families and private servants. The words "members of his family forming part of his household" in s.20(1)(b) of the 1978 Act should be given their normal meaning, the context being a reference to members of a sovereign's or head of state's household,[99b] not the household of a diplomatic agent.[100]

[98] cf. *Sultan of Johore v Abubakar* [1952] A.C. 318 where the Judicial Committee expressed the view that there had not been established any absolute rule that a foreign sovereign could not be impleaded in our courts.

[99] *Compania Naviera Vascongado v S.S. "Cristina"* [1938] A.C. 485 at 490.

[99a] The immunity does not extend to former heads of state (see *Zu Sayn-Wittgenstein-Sayn v Juan Carlos I* [2022] EWHC 668 (QB); [2022] 1 W.L.R. 3311 at [59]).

[99b] In *Zu Sayn-Wittgenstein-Sayn v Juan Carlos I* [2022] EWHC 668 (QB), the former King of Spain, who had abdicated, was held not to be a member of the new king's household for the purposes of the State Immunity Act 1978 (see [61]–[63]). The fact that the former king was not dependant on the current monarch and lived outside of Spain were identified by Nicklin J as a key factor in making this determination.

[100] *Apex Global Management Ltd v Fi Call Ltd* [2013] EWHC 587 (Ch) (it was observed that the purpose of the head of state's immunity was functional, likewise the personal immunity of a sovereign's family: it could not extend to everyone who assisted the sovereign or to everyone who carried out royal, constitutional or representational functions), upheld on appeal [2014] 1 W.L.R. 492, although the Court of Appeal took a narrower view of the definition of "household," as not including either a regent (unless the regent could be regarded as a head of state in their own right) or an heir (paragraph [40] per Briggs LJ).

7. Corporations, Trade Unions and Unincorporated Associations

Corporations, directors and members

Replace paragraph 3-52 with:

The directors of a limited company (or Plc), however, are not liable personally for the torts of the company's employees by reason of their position as directors,[141a] unless they were responsible for ordering the acts to be done or the omissions to be made or had assumed a personal duty of care.[142] They may, though, be liable, if there are facts from which an inference can be drawn that the relationship of principal and agent has been established between the directors and the company, but the mere fact of their being the sole directors and shareholders is insufficient.[143] Similarly, the members of a company, are not, as such, liable for torts committed by the company.[144] As a body corporate, it has a personality which is distinct from its members. Nevertheless, it cannot be doubted that an employee or agent, by whom a company commits a tort, is personally liable to the same extent as would be any other employee or agent who commits a tort in the service or on behalf of a principal or employer. Moreover a director of a company owes a common law duty of care to the company which is the same as that set out in s.214 of the Insolvency Act 1986.[145] 3-52

[141a] A director of a company who is also an employee of that company is owed the same duty of care by the company as an employee who is not a director (see *Carr v Brands Transport Ltd* [2022] EWHC 3167 (KB)).

[142] See *Williams v Natural Life Health Foods Ltd* [1998] 1 W.L.R. 830, HL; also *Hale v Guildarch Ltd* [1999] P.N.L.R. 44 (employees of a finance company not personally liable where they were taken not to have assumed personal responsibility for negligent advice which induced the claimants to enter a disastrous scheme, which involved their obtaining a loan secured on the equity of their home); also *Wragg v Partco Group Ltd* [2002] EWCA Civ 594, CA (directors' liability for alleged misstatement in the context of a company takeover). See Todd, "Liability of agents in tort" (1998) 3 P.N. 136.

[143] *Rainham Chemical Works v Belvedere Fish Guano Co* [1921] 2 A.C. 465; *Performing Right Soc. v Ciryl Syndicate* [1924] 1 K.B. 1.

[144] See, e.g. *Sweeney v Duggan* [1991] 2 I.R. 275 (majority shareholder not liable to an employee of the company whose judgment against the company remained unsatisfied after it went into liquidation: in the absence of special circumstances, the relationship between the parties was not of itself sufficiently proximate to justify imposing a duty of care and further, the claim, if allowed, would offend the rule that the defendant and the company were separate and distinct persons in law).

[145] *Re D'Jan of London; Copp v D'Jan* [1994] 1 B.C.L.C. 561.

17. JOINT AND SEVERAL TORTFEASORS

Contribution between tortfeasors

Replace footnote 308 with:

3-113 [308] Which came into force on 1 January 1979. The Act does not automatically apply to all contribution claims, but only to those contribution claims which are governed by English law (see *Roberts v Soldiers, Sailors, Airmen and Families Association* [2022] UKSC 29; [2023] P.I.Q.R. P7, where the Supreme Court held that the Act did not apply to a claim for contribution in a case governed by German law).

Replace footnote 313 with:

3-114 [313] Civil Liability (Contribution) Act 1978 s.1(4) and see *Percy v Merriman White (A Firm)* [2022] EWCA Civ 493; [2022] P.N.L.R. 20, where the Court of Appeal confirmed that the party seeking contribution had to demonstrate that the person from whom contribution was sought was liable, and that an attempt to foreclose this through a settlement agreement between the claimant and the party seeking contribution would, prima facie, deprive the party from whom contribution was sought of their rights under the European Convention on Human Rights art.6.

Replace footnote 316 with:

3-115 [316] This was applied in *Eastgate Group Ltd v Lindsey Morden Group Inc* [2001] EWCA Civ 1446; [2002] C.P. Rep. 7.

Replace footnote 317 with:

3-116 [317] Section 2(3) of the 1978 Act. In *A-R v Eljamel* [2022] CSIH 34; 2022 S.L.T. 881, the Inner House of the Court of Session upheld an apportionment of 100% contribution by one defendant, on the basis that the negligence of the other defendant had very small causative potency and limited moral blameworthiness.

Chapter 4

PRINCIPAL DEFENCES AND DISCHARGES FROM LIABILITY

Table of Contents

1. Contributory Negligence

Motor accidents

Replace footnote 179 with:

[179] *Eagle v Chambers (No.1)* [2003] EWCA Civ 1107; [2004] R.T.R. 9 at [16], per Hale LJ and see *Jackson v Murray* [2015] UKSC 5; [2015] 2 All E.R. 805 at [39]–[43], per Lord Reed. See further, e.g. *Adams v Gibson* [2016] EWHC 3209 (QB) (claimant one third at fault where he failed to look to his right before crossing the road and chose not to use a nearby pedestrian crossing). See also *Cameron v Nwankwo* [2022] CSOH 7 where the contributory negligence of a pedestrian who, at night and whilst wearing dark clothing, had chosen to cross a four-lane carriageway at a place where there was no traffic light control or central pedestrian refuge, despite there being a nearby pedestrian crossing, was assessed at one-third. **4-59**

Illustrations

Replace footnote 226 with:

[226] *Brumder v Motornet Service and Repairs Ltd* [2013] EWCA Civ 195; [2013] B.C.C. 381. In contrast see *Carr v Brands Transport Ltd* [2022] EWHC 3167 (KB), where a claim brought by the executive director of the defendant was not defeated by the *Brumder* principle, because the claimant was not the sole author of their own misfortune. **4-75**

3. LIMITATION OF ACTION

(A) General principles

Delay in bringing action

Replace footnote 532 with:

4-167 [532] *Khan v RM Falvey & Co* [2002] EWCA Civ 400; [2002] P.N.L.R. 28; applied in *West Wallasey Car Hire Ltd v Berkson & Berkson (A Firm)* [2010] P.N.L.R. 14 QBD (Birmingham) (a claim against solicitors and counsel for failing to advise that an earlier action was flawed, failed, where damage was suffered when the earlier proceedings were commenced, not at the time when they were being determined). See also *Hatton v Chafes (A Firm)* [2003] EWCA Civ 341; [2003] P.N.L.R. 24; *Berney v Saul* [2013] EWCA Civ 640; [2013] P.N.L.R. 26 (a claimant who alleged negligence by her former solicitors in failing to serve Particulars of Claim within the time allowed by the Rules suffered actual damage for limitation purposes from the time when the defendant's solicitors withdrew an earlier concession that no point would be taken on delay and said that an application to serve Particulars of Claim out of time would have to be made: from that time there was a real risk that the claim would have to be settled with a discount for the chance that time would not be extended if the application was made); *Christie v Mary Ward Legal Centre* [2022] EWHC 1684 (QB); [2022] P.N.L.R. 25 (actual damage was suffered at the date of sale of a property rather than the date on which a possession order was made, because until the time of the sale the claimant could have sought relief).

(C) Latent damage

ILLUSTRATIONS

Replace paragraph 4-242 with:

4-242 Where the claimant sued on a negligent survey report, but had been aware at the time of some defects in the building not mentioned by the surveyor, it was held that so far as other defects were concerned, discovered several years later, he was not debarred from relying on the extended limitation period.[806] However, time ran against a claimant bringing a claim in negligence against structural engineers who had given advice in relation to the construction of a waterproofed basement room at the claimant's home, from the date when serious flooding into the room occurred.[807] Where the claimant alleged his solicitors had been negligent in failing to advise him about the effect of acquiring property with another under a joint tenancy, it was not the case that for time to run against him, he needed to know that the solicitors owed him a legal duty to advise that the joint tenancy was unilaterally severable; and the fact that he did not turn his mind to the damage having been attributable to the solicitor's omission was not fatal to his knowledge under s.14A(8)(A).[808] Nor did the defence succeed where consulting actuaries had failed to give adequate advice in relation to a client's purchase of a with-profits policy of annuity from the Equitable Life Assurance Society: annual statements from the Society which on a close reading were capable of informing the client of the correct position were insufficient to give knowledge for purposes of s.14A, where the defendant's advice had over the years conditioned him to consider that he did not need to read them closely.[809] Where it was alleged that solicitors failed to advise the claimants that if they failed to file an objection to registration of a title to land by a certain date an adjudicator to HM Land Registry would have a statutory discretion whether or not to close the title, the "material fact about the damage" of which the claimants had to have knowledge for time to run under s.14A(6), was not the solicitors' failure to file an objection before the deadline, but that the effect of that failure was to allow a discretionary decision to be made against them in relation to the title.[810] In *PSGS Trust Corp Ltd v Aon UK Ltd*,[810a] Miles J refused summary judgment on a limitation basis as it was arguable that the claimants could rely on s.14A to extend the limitation period in respect of advice about the design of schemes of arrangement that sought to restructure a pension scheme.

[806] *Felton v Gaskill Osborne & Co* [1993] 43 E.G. 118.

[807] *Renwick v Simon and Michael Brooke Architects* [2011] EWHC 874 (TCC); [2011] P.N.L.R. 31 (it was said to be at least arguable that a different cause of action, later in time, arose when the engineers gave allegedly negligent advice in relation to the use of internal rendering as a form of remedy for water penetration and the solution failed).

[808] *Boycott v Perrins Guy Williams* [2011] EWHC 2969 (Ch); [2012] P.N.L.R. 25, para.4-162.

[809] *Andrews v Barnett Waddingham* [2006] P.N.L.R. 24 (time ran from a later point when the defendant wrote to the client warning of the danger that the future profits of a with-profits annuity would be less than expected; appeal, on a different point, allowed [2006] EWCA Civ 93; [2006] P.N.L.R. 24).

[810] *Blakemores LDP (In Administration) v Scott* [2015] EWCA Civ 999; [2016] C.P. Rep. 1.

[810a] *PSGS Trust Corp Ltd v Aon UK Ltd* [2022] EWHC 2058 (Ch); [2023] P.N.L.R. 2.

(D) Miscellaneous limitation periods

Periods of limitation prescribed by other Acts

Human Rights Act 1998

Replace footnote 826 with:

[826] Human Rights Act 1998 s.7(5). In *CJ v Chief Constable of Wiltshire* [2022] EWHC 1661 (QB); [2023] P.I.Q.R. P2, Martin Spencer J extended time to bring a claim under s.7(5). Factors taken into account were as follows; the court would be slow to find that a claim involving serious sexual assaults was time-barred; that where the claimants were children the court would take the fact of their minority as an important factor in exercising its discretion, particularly as the period under the Limitation Act would not begin to run whilst the claimant was under the disability of minority; that in this case the delay was not unreasonable, as the claimants would not have known that they had viable claims until disciplinary proceedings against the investigating officer had been completed in 2017, and would not be prejudicial to the Chief Constable. **4-248**

4. OTHER DEFENCES

(A) Illegality

Consistency within the law

Replace footnote 911 with:

[911] *Ellis v Counties Manukau District Health Board* [2007] 1 N.Z.L.R. 196; and see *Hunter Area Health Service v Presland* [2005] NSWCA 33; (2005) 63 N.S.W.L.R. 22. See *Lewis-Ranwell v G4S Health Services UK Ltd* [2022] EWHC 1213 (QB); [2022] P.I.Q.R. P16 and *Traylor v Kent and Medway NHS Social Care Partnership Trust* [2022] EWHC 260 (QB); [2022] P.I.Q.R. P12, see para.4-287a. **4-282**

Gradations of personal responsibility

After paragraph 4-287, add new paragraph:

In *Lewis-Ranwell v G4S Health Services (UK) Ltd*,[923a] the claimant had been found not guilty by reason of insanity following his killing of three people whilst in a delusional state. Prior to the killings, the claimant had been released on police bail after being examined by staff employed by the defendants. The claimant brought a claim for damages on the basis that the defendants had negligently as- **4-287a** sessed him. The defendants sought to strike out the claim on the basis of illegality. Garnham J refused to strike out the claim, holding that where a claimant was found not guilty by reason of insanity then the doctrine of illegality would not apply because the claimant was a fortiori unaware that their actions were wrong and therefore there was no criminal or quasi-criminal conduct on which to found the illegality defence. Further, Garnham J held that allowing such a claim to proceed would not be legally incoherent or harmful to the integrity of the legal system, notwithstanding that at the same time the claimant would potentially be liable in tort in respect of his actions.[923b]

[923a] *Lewis-Ranwell v G4S Health Services (UK) Ltd* [2022] EWHC 1213 (QB).

[923b] In *Traylor v Kent and Medway NHS Social Care Partnership Trust* [2022] EWHC 260 (QB), Johnson J, obiter, reached a similar conclusion in a case where the claimant had been found not guilty by reason of insanity in relation to an incident where he had stabbed his daughter during a psychotic episode. Johnson J held that the application of the illegality defence in tort in circumstances where the claimant had been found insane (and therefore found to not know that the act was illegal) by a criminal court would not be inconsistent with the authorities that indicate that, for the illegality defence to apply, the claimant should know that they were acting unlawfully. Johnson J rejected an argument that because the Criminal Injuries Compensation Scheme pays compensation in circumstances where a person would have been the victim of a "crime of violence" but for the insanity verdict then the claimant should be treated as if he had been convicted of a criminal offence for the purposes of the illegality defence in tort.

Illustrations

Replace paragraph 4-327 with:

4-327 A recent decision involving dangerous driving well illustrates the weighing of degrees of turpitude. In *RO v Gray*[972] the claimant and the defendant were involved in altercations over a short period and which were started by the claimant and his passenger. His conduct included threats of violence, hitting another car and attacking a passenger, and was described by the judge as "deplorable and disgraceful". But the judge also considered that its gravity was closer to the bottom of the range than the top, and could be categorised as relatively minor and not uncommon criminality. The defendant, however, deliberately rammed the claimant's car at speed, causing a major crash and life-changing injuries for the claimant. The defendant was prosecuted and sentenced to more than three years in prison, whereas the claimant was not prosecuted. The judge concluded that it would be wholly disproportionate to refuse relief and would be contrary to any sensible notion of public interest, putting the claimant in the position of an outlaw. Similarly, in *Cojanu v Essex Partnership University NHS Trust*,[972a] Ritchie J held that the illegality defence would not apply to a situation where carelessness by an NHS Trust had resulted in a prisoner suffering more serious consequences from injuries sustained during an assault that he had perpetrated than would otherwise have been suffered. The judge held that there was no connection between the crime and the civil claim and to bar recovery on the basis of illegality would "take away the force and effect of the decisions of Parliament to grant convicted and unconvicted persons in prison the equivalent rights to NHS care as are afforded to other members of the public."[972b]

[972] *RO v Gray* [2021] EWHC 2770 (QB); [2022] R.T.R. 15.

[972a] *Cojanu v Essex Partnership University NHS Trust* [2022] EWHC 197 (QB); [2022] 4 W.L.R. 33.

[972b] *Cojanu v Essex Partnership University NHS Trust* [2022] EWHC 197 (QB) at [103].

(B) Abuse of process

Statutory intervention

Replace footnote 985 with:

[985] Dishonesty is to be judged according to the test set out by the Supreme Court in *Ivey v Genting Casinos Ltd (t/a Crockfords Club)* [2017] UKSC 67; [2018] A.C. 391 at [62], [74]. For an application of the *Ivey* test to s.57 see *Patel v Arriva Midlands Ltd* [2019] EWHC 1216 (QB); [2019] 1 W.L.R. 6598 (claimant was fundamentally dishonest when he and his son presented to experts that he could not walk, communicate or manage for himself, despite knowing that he could). The claimant's dishonesty must have a substantial effect on the presentation of the claim and dishonesty as to matters incidental or collateral to the claim are not fundamental for the purposes of the defence (see *Cojanu v Essex Partnership University NHS Trust* [2022] EWHC 197 (QB)). **4-335**

Chapter 5

CAUSATION AND REMOTENESS OF DAMAGE

Table of Contents

2. Cause in Fact

(A) "But for" causation

Bonnington Castings Ltd v Wardlaw

Replace paragraph 5-20 with:

The Privy Council applied *Bonnington Castings* to consecutive causes in *Williams v The Bermuda Hospitals Board*.[48] In this case the claimant had suffered injury to his heart and lungs as a result of sepsis resulting from appendicitis. The sepsis developed incrementally over the six-hour period between hospital admission and operation. Part of this time was a negligent delay. The non-negligent and negligent periods of time operated as consecutive and cumulative causes of the totality of the sepsis. Each period had made a material contribution to the totality of the septic process, and therefore, on the balance of probabilities the delay had made a material contribution to the injury to the heart and lungs. Again, in *John v* **5-20**

Central Manchester and Manchester Children's University Hospitals NHS Foundation Trust[49] a negligent delay in treatment was seen as making a material contribution to the totality of the cognitive and neurophysiological injury suffered by the claimant in circumstances where the negligent factor was the second in a series of three matters that contributed to the damage. The claimant non-negligently fell down stairs and suffered a negligent delay in treatment and a non-negligent post-operative infection, all of which led to raised inter-cranial pressure. Taken together, the sequence of events led to the claimant suffering from the raised inter-cranial pressure, and therefore each event had made a material contribution to the injury. Obiter, in *CNZ v Royal Bath Hospitals NHS Foundation Trust*,[49a] Ritchie J held that, had the claimant's injuries been caused by a combination of negligent and non-negligent profound hypoxic ischaemia (PHI) then the claimant would have been able to establish that each minute of negligent PHI after the non-negligent PHI made a material contribution to her injuries. Whilst in principle damages could be apportioned on the basis of a comparison between negligent and non-negligent PHI, medical science could not provide a fair a reasonable method for apportionment and the claimant was therefore entitled to recover 100% of the damages representing the loss suffered.

[48] *Williams v Bermuda Hospitals Board* [2016] UKPC 4; [2016] A.C. 888; C. Hobson, "Williams v The Bermuda Hospitals Board: pro-patient, but for ambiguities which remain" (2017) 25 M.L.R. 126; Stapleton and Steel, "Causes and contributions" (2016) 132 L.Q.R. 363.

[49] *John v Central Manchester and Manchester Children's University Hospitals NHS Foundation Trust* [2016] EWHC 407 (QB); [2016] 4 W.L.R. 54.

[49a] *CNZ v Royal Bath Hospitals NHS Foundation Trust* [2023] EWHC 19 (KB).

(D) Loss of a chance

Claimant's hypothetical conduct

Replace footnote 136 with:

5-68 [136] *Sellars v Adelaide Petroleum NL* (1994) 179 C.L.R. 332 at 353; *Allied Maples Group Ltd v Simmons & Simmons* [1995] 1 W.L.R. 1602, 1610; *Benton v Miller & Poulgrain* [2005] 1 N.Z.L.R. 66 at [47]–[49] N.Z.C.A.; *Wellesley Partners LLP v Withers LLP* [2015] EWCA Civ 1146; [2016] 2 W.L.R. 1351 at [98]; *Perry v Raleys Solicitors* [2019] UKSC 5; [2020] A.C. 352 at [20]. See also *Levicom International Holdings BV v Linklaters* [2010] P.N.L.R. 29 (where a client consults top-tier solicitors the presumption is that he will follow any non-negligent advice that should have been given). See also *Coote v Ullstein* [2022] EWHC 607 (QB), where the court's broad-brush assessment of the loss of chance included an assessment of the chances that a claimant would have been granted funding by the Legal Services Commission.

3. THE DUTY NEXUS QUESTION

Khan v Meadows

After "born with autism.", add new footnote 172a:

5-91 [172a] The decision in *Khan* was applied in *D v Grampian Health Board* [2022] CSOH 63 at [173]–[174], which held that there was no sufficient nexus between breaches of duty and the adverse outcome.

5. Remoteness of Damage

(C) Application of the foresight test

(i) Personal injuries

Hughes v Lord Advocate

Replace footnote 290 with:

[290] *Hughes v Lord Advocate* [1963] A.C. 837 at 858, per Lord Pearson; *Hadlow v Peterborough City Council* [2011] EWCA Civ 1329 (teacher working in a secure unit for violent women was wrongly left alone with three such women and tripped over a chair when rapidly leaving the room: defendant liable even though the injury did not come about by an attack or threat but by the claimant's action in response to the risk from her situation). See also *Hill v Ministry of Justice* [2022] EWHC 370 (QB). **5-146**

Chapter 6

PROOF AND DAMAGES

Table of Contents

3. Heads of Damages and their Assessment

(B) Damage to chattels, land and buildings

(i) Damage to chattels

Credit car hire

After paragraph 6-92, add new paragraph:

In *Armstead v Royal Sun Alliance Insurance Co Ltd*,[335a] the claimant entered into a credit hire agreement following an accident. Whilst driving the hire car it was involved in an accident and damaged. The credit hire agreement included a clause that required the hirer to pay a fee whilst a damaged hire car was undergoing repair. This could not be recovered from the insurers of the vehicle involved in the original accident,[335b] as a contractual arrangement could not be the basis for the recovery of economic loss and was too remote to be recoverable. The damages arising under **6-92a** the contractual arrangement were to be distinguished from the costs of repairing the damage to the hire car and any consequential economic loss, which were recoverable by the claimant as a bailee.

335a *Armstead v Royal Sun Alliance Insurance Co Ltd* [2022] EWCA Civ 497; [2022] R.T.R. 23.

335b *Armstead v Royal Sun Alliance Insurance Co Ltd* [2022] EWCA Civ 497 at [52]–[57].

(C) Damages for personal injuries

(v) Provisional damages and interim awards

Provisional damages

After paragraph 6-180, add new paragraph:

6-180a In the event that the claimant who has been granted a provisional damages order dies as a result of damage caused by the negligence that led to the order being made, then the estate of the claimant will be able to apply for further damages to be awarded under the order. In *Power v Bernard Hastie & Co Ltd*, a provisional damages order had been made in 1991 for the benefit of a claimant who had been exposed to asbestos, resulting in early asbestosis and asymptomatic pleural plaques.[613a] In 2017 the claimant died, allegedly because of asbestos related conditions, and his executor applied to the court to be substituted in place of the claimant in order to pursue an application for further damages. Johnson J held that the statutory framework did not prevent an application for further damages being made by the executor of an injured person's estate if the right to make that application had passed to the executor and the claimant's right to apply for further damages had been vested in claimant at the time of his death and had survived for the benefit of his estate by operation of s.1 of the Law Reform (Miscellaneous Provisions) Act 1934. Johnson J also rejected an argument that the Limitation Act 1980 applied to an application for further damages, holding that the application was not an action for damages in respect of personal injuries under s.11 and that the time period within which an application for further damages was to be made would be prescribed by the award of provisional damages itself.

613a *Power v Bernard Hastie & Co Ltd* [2022] EWHC 1927 (QB); [2022] P.I.Q.R. Q5.

Chapter 7

VICARIOUS LIABILITY AND NON-DELEGABLE DUTIES

Table of Contents

1. Vicarious Liability

(D) Relationships analogous to employment

Employer and independent contractor

Replace paragraph 7-49 with:

Prior to *Barclays* there were a number of indications that the distinction between employees on the one hand and independent contractors on the other was not affected by the decisions imposing vicarious liability outside the simple relationship of employment.[88] In particular, in *Kafagi v JBW Group Ltd*[89] the Court of Appeal held that the defendant company, which was in the business of collecting council tax debts, was not vicariously liable for the actions of a sub-contractor. Given the characteristics of the sub-contractor's business, the sub-contractor was more like a competitor of the business of the defendant than a person integrated into the business. There was not even a vestigial degree of control of the type contemplated in *Cox*. Similarly, the healthcare services in a prison were not sufficiently integrated into the enterprise of running the prison to render the prison governor vicariously liable for the actions of the healthcare provider.[90] Again, a firm providing nightclub security was not vicariously liable for the actions of a doorman employed by a sub-contractor, given that the doorman was neither controlled by the firm, nor integrated 7-49 into their business.[91] Likewise, the relationship between a bank and an independent financial advisor who recommended their products did not give rise to vicarious liability despite the close commercial relationship between them. The bank and the advisor were separate businesses carrying out separate functions.[92]

[88] See, for example, *E v English Province of Our Lady of Charity* [2012] EWCA Civ 938 at [69]; *Woodland v Swimming Teachers Association* [2013] UKSC 66; [2014] A.C. 537 at [3]; *Ng Huat Seng v Madni* [2017] SGCA 58 at [63]–[64].

[89] *Kafagi v JBW Group Ltd* [2018] EWCA Civ 1157, which was expressly approved by the Supreme Court in *Barclays Bank Plc v Various Claimants* [2020] UKSC 13 at [25]. See also *Anderson v Sense Network Ltd* [2018] EWHC 2834 (Comm) (defendant financial services company not vicariously liable for torts committed by the employees of an appointed representative: the appointed representative was a recognisably independent business, and the torts of its employees were attributable to it alone).

[90] *Razumas v Ministry of Justice* [2018] EWHC 215 (QB); [2018] P.I.Q.R. P10 at [174]–[176].

[91] *Davis v Fessey* unreported 5 April 2018 QBD. See also *Kalma v African Minerals Ltd* [2018] EWHC 3506 (QB) (defendant not vicariously liable for the acts of Sierra Leone police officers, as these officers performed duties which extended far beyond the narrow parameters of the business activity of the defendant).

[92] *Barness v Ingenious Media Ltd* [2019] EWHC 3299 (Ch); [2020] P.N.L.R. 10.

After paragraph 7-49, add new paragraphs:

7-49a **Independent contractors and relationships akin to employment post-Barclays** Following *Barclays*, a number of cases have considered whether there are any circumstances in which an independent contractor can be found to be in a relationship akin to employment with the defendant for whom they perform services. In *SKX v Manchester City Council*, a local authority was not vicariously liable where it had placed the claimant in a privately-owned children's home, and the chief executive of the home sexually abused him. The executive had not been in a relationship akin to employment with the local authorities which placed children in the care homes he managed. Moreover, he had been carrying out an independent business on behalf of a third party, namely the company which operated those homes, which was neither a part of the authority's organisation nor integrated into its structure.[93] Similarly, in *Blackpool Football Club Ltd v DSN*, a football club was not vicariously liable for the actions of an unpaid scout. The scout carried out activities that were important to the football club, but carried them out independently and without control of the club, leading to the conclusion that the scout was not in a relationship akin to employment.[94] In *Hughes v Rattan* the relationship between a dental practice and self-employed associate dentists working at the practice also was not akin to employment, the most significant factors pointing to this conclusion being the associate dentists' freedom to work at the practice for as many or as few hours as they wished and their freedom to work for other practices or businesses.[95] In *Carr v Brands Transport Ltd*, the relationship between the defendant logistics business and their transport manager, who worked for the defendant, and many other logistics businesses, under a contract for services and rendered monthly invoices, was not a relationship akin to employment, and therefore the defendant was not vicariously liable for his negligence.[95a]

[93] *SKX v Manchester City Council* [2021] EWHC 782 (QB); [2021] 4 W.L.R. 56.

[94] *Blackpool Football Club Ltd v DSN* [2021] EWCA Civ 1352. For a commentary on this case, see Allison Silink and Desmond Ryan, "The relevance of 'control' in both stages of the test for vicarious liability in relationships that are 'akin to employment': an analysis of Blackpool in the Court of Appeal" (2022) 38(4) P.N. 229–238. Similarly, in *TVZ v Manchester City Football Club Ltd* [2022] EWHC 7

(QB), an unpaid scout and unpaid coach of youth football teams who represented that these teams acted as "feeder clubs" for the defendant was not in a relationship akin to employment with the defendants. Whilst the club had provided the coach with significant perks that appeared to confirm his connection with the club, he had complete autonomy in respect of the planning, running, administration and financing of the teams he coached and the club did not have even a vestigial degree of control.

[95] *Hughes v Rattan* [2022] EWCA Civ 107; [2022] 1 W.L.R. 1680 at [84]–[91]. For a commentary see Christine Beuermann, "Strict liability for the torts of associate dentists" (2022) 38(3) P.N. 166–173.

[95a] *Carr v Brands Transport Ltd* [2022] EWHC 3167 (KB).

Relationship not akin to employment when the tortfeasor is not an independent contractor In *MXX v A Secondary School*,[95b] HH Judge Wall (sitting as a judge of the High Court) held that a tortfeasor who was undertaking a one week work experience placement (which was a compulsory part of the tortfeasors college course) at the defendant school was not in a relationship akin to employment with the school. The tortfeasor had asked to spend the week at the school as a favour, was 18 and was unqualified. The school did not derive any benefit from the placement (and, in fact, the placement imposed a burden on the school as a person on placement had to be supervised at all times) and the tortfeasor had no responsibilities during the placement. It was, therefore, not fair, just or reasonable to conclude that this placement was akin to employment. 7-49b

[95b] *MXX v A Secondary School* [2022] EWHC 2207 (QB).

2. NON-DELEGABLE DUTIES

(A) Introduction

Primary duties

After "the contractor's work.", add new footnote 219a:

[219a] For consideration of pleading issues in non-delegable duty cases, see *Gulf View Medical Centre Ltd v Tesheira* [2022] UKPC 38. 7-106

(C) Protective relationships

Identifying factors

Replace paragraph 7-112 with:

The five factors identified by Lord Sumption in establishing a personal duty of this kind were the vulnerability of the claimant, the existence of a relationship between the claimant and the defendant by virtue of which the defendant had a degree of protective custody and control over the claimant, the claimant having no control over how the defendant chose to perform its obligations, the delegation of that custody and control to another person, and negligence by that person in the performance of the very function assumed by the defendant and delegated to him or her.[240] A clear instance was the non-delegable duty of an employer to maintain a safe system of work.[241] And in his Lordship's opinion the time had come to recognise that the relationships between hospitals and their patients,[242] and local education authorities and their pupils[243] fell into the same category.[244] In *Woodland* itself, applying the above principles, the duty of a local education authority was held to be non-delegable in circumstances where a pupil suffered serious injury in the course of a school swimming lesson conducted by swimming instructors provided by an independent contractor.[245] 7-112

240 *Woodland v Essex CC* [2013] UKSC 66; [2014] A.C. 537 at [23].

241 *Wilsons & Clyde Coal Co Ltd v English* [1938] A.C. 57 (HL); *McDermid v Nash Dredging and Reclamation Co Ltd* [1987] A.C. 906 (HL); *Kondis v State Transport Authority* (1984) 154 C.L.R. 672. For consideration of the employer's duties as non-delegable duties in circumstances where the employee's injuries resulted from the negligence of an independent contractor engaged to perform the duties of a transport manager for a logistics company, see *Carr v Brands Transport Ltd* [2022] EWHC 3167 (KB) at [278]–[307], see also para.7-49.

242 Approving the approach of Lord Greene MR in *Gold v Essex CC* [1942] 2 K.B. 293 CA at 301 and of Denning LJ in *Cassidy v Ministry of Health* [1951] 2 K.B. 343 CA at 359–365; and see *X (Minors) v Bedfordshire CC* [1995] 2 A.C. 633 HL at 740; *Robertson v Nottingham HA* [1997] 8 Med L.R. 1 CA (Civ Div) at 13. See generally P. Giliker "Non-delegable duties and institutional liability for the negligence of hospital staff: fair, just and reasonable?" (2017) 33 P.N. 109. See also the decision of the Supreme Court of Ireland in *Morrissey v Health Service Executive* [2020] IESC 6; [2020] P.N.L.R. 17 at [13.1]–[13-26] (the Health Service Executive owed a non-delegable duty to a patient in respect of cancer screening services provided by an independent contractor). Contrast *Hopkins v Akramy* [2020] EWHC 3445; [2021] Q.B. 564 (hospital trust did not owe a non-delegable duty of care in relation to medical services provided by an agency when the imposition of that duty was inconsistent with the statutory framework governing the relationship) and see further, Ch.10, para.10-175.

243 The category is well recognised by the High Court of Australia: *Commonwealth v Introvigne* (1982) 150 C.L.R. 258; *New South Wales v Lepore* [2003] HCA 4; (2003) 212 C.L.R. 511 per Gaudron, McHugh, Gummow and Hayne JJ.

244 His Lordship said other examples were likely to be prisoners and residents in care homes. In *GB v Home Office* [2015] EWHC 819 (QB) a detainee who had received medical treatment in an immigration removal centre run by an independent organisation on behalf of the United Kingdom Home Office was held to be owed a non-delegable duty of care. In *Hughes v Rattan* [2022] EWCA Civ 107; [2022] 1 W.L.R. 1680, a dental practice was held to owe a non-delegable duty of care to a patient of the practice in respect of alleged negligence by self-employed associate dentists at the practice. For a commentary see Christine Beuermann, "Strict liability for the torts of associate dentists" (2022) 38(3) P.N. 166–173.

245 The case was remitted for trial, and in *Woodland v Maxwell* [2015] EWHC 273 (QB) the claimant established that her injuries were caused both by a lifeguard employed at the pool and by a teacher in failing to notice that she was in difficulties in the water.

CHAPTER 8

THE STANDARD OF CARE

TABLE OF CONTENTS

1. THE REASONABLE CARE STANDARD GENERALLY

Reasonableness

Replace paragraph 8-06 with:

Nevertheless, although the standard is impersonal it does not wholly disregard the circumstances of the individual. When considering the standard of care required of a reasonable driver it may be irrelevant that the driver is male or female, a learner or experienced,[8] but it is not irrelevant if the driver is suffering from an illness of which they are unaware, and which affects their ability to drive.[9] Although a defendant who is merely impaired by medical problems, whether physical or mental, cannot escape liability if their actions, however irrational, caused injury by failing to exercise reasonable care.[10] When considering the standard required of a reasonably competent medical practitioner, the specialism within which the individual practised must be taken into account,[11] although not the extent of their experience in that specialism.[12] In *Arthur Guinness, Son & Co (Dublin) Ltd v Owners of the Motor Vessel Freshfield (The Lady Gwendolen)*,[13] a well-known brewing company was liable for failing properly to supervise the master of a vessel in their ownership, which collided with another vessel in thick fog. Winn LJ said that the law, "must apply a standard which is not relaxed to cater for their factual ignorance of all activities outside brewing: having become owners of ships, they must behave as reasonable shipowners."[14] Where the party alleged to have been culpable is a child it has been said that the question is whether the child's conduct fell below a standard that should objectively be expected of a child of that age. For a child to be culpable it would have to be careless to a very high degree.[15] The position was summarised by Jackson LJ in *FB v Rana*:[15a] **8-06**

> "From the defendant's point of view, it is harsh to disregard their limitations and to hold them liable for doing that which they could not help doing or for failing to achieve that which they could not achieve. But a claimant is entitled to expect that those whom he or

she encounters in the ordinary transactions of life will adhere to certain general standards. Thus in *Nettleship v Weston* [1971] Q.B. 691 the Court of Appeal held that a learner driver should be judged by the standards of a competent and experienced driver. In effect, the law of tort achieves a compromise. It takes account of those characteristics which cannot be ignored (for example that the defendant was a child or was blind), but subject to that it imposes a general duty of care upon all members of society, which is not tailored to their individual strengths and weaknesses."

[8] *Nettleship v Weston* [1971] 2 Q.B. 691 CA (Civ Div); Ch.11, para.11-281.

[9] *Mansfield v Weetabix Ltd* [1998] 1 W.L.R. 1263 CA (Civ Div) where a lorry driver caused extensive property damage on account of his ability to drive having been impaired by malignant insulinoma, of which he was unaware, and which caused a gradual hypoglaecimic state. The standard of care such a driver was obliged to show to other road users was that which was to be expected of a reasonably competent driver unaware that they were or might be suffering from a condition that impaired their ability to drive. To apply an objective standard in a way that did not take account of such a condition would be to apply a test of strict liability. Since the driver did not know and could not reasonably have known of the infirmity which caused the accident, he was not at fault and was not negligent; per Legatt LJ at 1267G–1267H, 1268D–1268E. Contrast *Dunnage v Randall* [2015] EWCA Civ 673; [2016] Q.B. 639.

[10] *Dunnage v Randall* [2016] Q.B. 639 (where the claimant's uncle, who suffered from schizophrenia, was liable for setting himself on fire and thereby causing injury to the claimant who attempted to rescue him).

[11] See, e.g. *SC (A Child) v University Hospital Southampton NHS Foundation Trust* [2020] EWHC 1610 (QB) (consultant negligent in failing to treat a child for meningitis, whereas a Senior House Officer was not). See also *XM v Leicestershire Partnership NHS Trust* [2020] EWHC 3102 (QB).

[12] *Djemal v Bexley HA* [1995] Med. L.R. 269 (the standard of care to be applied was that of a reasonably competent senior house officer acting as a casualty officer regardless of length of experience); and see *Wilsher v Essex AHA* [1987] Q.B. 730; [1987] 2 W.L.R. 425 and *FB v Rana*; sub nom. *FB v Princess Alexandra Hospital NHS Trust* [2017] EWCA Civ 334; [2017] P.I.Q.R. P17 (no difference in the standard of care required of an accident and emergency (A&E) senior house officer as compared to a more senior doctor in the context of taking a patient history in A&E; per Lord Jackson at [46] and [59]).

[13] *Arthur Guinness, Son & Co (Dublin) Ltd v Owners of the Motor Vessel Freshfield (The Lady Gwendolen)* [1965] P. 294; [1965] 3 W.L.R. 91 CA.

[14] *Arthur Guinness, Son & Co (Dublin) Ltd v Owners of the Motor Vessel Freshfield (The Lady Gwendolen)* [1965] P. 294 at 350.

[15] *Orchard v Lee* [2009] EWCA Civ 295; [2009] P.I.Q.R. P16, see para.8-27 (13-year-old boy not liable to a school lunchtime supervisor, who was injured when the boy collided with her as he played a game of tag. The claim failed as no ordinarily prudent and reasonable 13-year-old boy playing tag in the relevant area of the school would reasonably have foreseen the risk of injury). See also *Zanner v Zanner* [2010] NSWCA 343 (an 11-year-old boy was negligent in manoeuvring the family car into a carport and running over his mother).

[15a] *FB v Rana* [2017] EWCA Civ 334 at [46].

2. MATTERS TAKEN INTO ACCOUNT

(C) Gravity of the consequences

Sporting activities

Participants in sport

Replace paragraph 8-27 with:

8-27 There is no rule of law that in order to succeed in an action against a fellow competitor the claimant must prove the defendant guilty of some reckless disregard for his or her safety.[65a] The standard of care that is expected is reasonable care in relation to the activity in question, taking into account the risks of the activity, the exigencies of the moment and all the circumstances of the case.[66] The standard is an objective one but can reflect the skill to be required of participants who operate within their sport at different levels: "there will ... be a higher degree of care required of a player in a First Division football match than of a player in a local league football match."[67] But liability was not established where two fellow jockeys left insufficient room for a pursuing horse to come along the inside rail, as a result of which the horse fell and the claimant, on a following horse, sustained serious injury: there was no liability for errors of judgment, lapses or oversights of which any participant might be guilty in the context of a fast-moving contest.[68] Similar considerations have applied to injuries suffered while the victims were water-skiing,[69] playing golf,[70] playing games of tag,[71] and even ballroom dancing.[72] In contrast, a jockey was negligent when he rode with a reckless disregard for another jockey's safety during a flat race: he had steered his mount into the path of the other horse, causing three horses and four riders to fall.[72a] Although jockeys need to be able to assess and reassess situations and make split-second decisions as to what to do, based on skill, experience and intuition, this was not a case of a simple lapse of concentration or momentary inattentiveness. It was however emphasised that the threshold for liability in such a case would be a high one and that each case must be determined on its own facts.[72b]

[65a] *Caldwell v Maguire* [2001] EWCA Civ 1054; [2002] P.I.Q.R. P6. In *Fulham Football Club v Jones* [2022] EWHC 1108 (QB), the trial judge materially misdirected himself in finding that "red card" breaches of the rules amounting to serious foul play and which endangered the safety of an opponent "would very likely amount to negligence". According to the Rules of the Game of Association Football such "red card" breaches were judged to be at least reckless and possibly deliberate: aligning serious foul play with actionable negligence wrongly reduced the ambit of the inquiry needed to answer the question of whether the tackle was not only a breach of the rules, but also negligent.

[66] *Wilks v Cheltenham Homeguard Motor Cycle & Light Car Club* [1971] 1 W.L.R. 668 CA (Civ Div) at 673–674; *Evans v Waitemata District Pony Club* [1972] N.Z.L.R. 773 at 775–776; *McComiskey v McDermott* [1974] I.R. 75; *Condon v Basi* [1985] 1 W.L.R. 866 at 868 CA (Civ Div); *Caldwell v Maguire* [2002] P.I.Q.R. P6; *Blake v Galloway* [2004] EWCA Civ 814; [2004] 1 W.L.R. 2844.

[67] *Condon v Basi* [1985] 1 W.L.R. 866 at 868, per Sir John Donaldson MR (a foul tackle by the defendant during a game of soccer broke the claimant's leg). See also *Watson v Gray*, *Times*, 26 November 1998 QBD; *McCord v Swansea City AFC Ltd*, *Times*, 11 February 1997 QBD; *Sharp v Highland and Islands Fire Board*, 2005 S.L.T. 855; 2005 S.C.L.R. 1049 OH; and see Khan and Wolfgarten, "Liability for Foul Play" 129 S.J. 859; McEwan, "Playing the Game: Negligence in Sport" 130 S.J. 581; Toczek, "A case of foul play" 152 N.L.J. 868; D. McArdle, "The enduring legacy of 'reckless disregard'" 34 C.L.W.R. 316.

[68] *Fairchild v Glenhaven Funeral Services Ltd (t/a GH Dovener & Son)* [2002] UKHL 22; [2002] P.I.Q.R. P28; D. McArdle and M.D. James, "Are you experienced? 'Playing cultures', sporting rules and personal injury litigation after Caldwell v Maguire" (2005) 13 Tort L.R.193.

[69] *Rootes v Shelton* [1968] A.L.R. 33 HC.

[70] *Potter v Carlisle and Cliftonville Golf Club Ltd* [1939] N.I. 114; *Brewer v Delo* [1967] 1 Lloyd's Rep. 488 QBD; *Ellison v Rogers* [1968] 1 O.R. 501; *Clark v Welsh* [1975] (4) S.A. 484; *Feeney v Lyall* [1991] S.L.T. 156 OH; *Lewis v Buckpool Golf Club*, 1993 S.L.T. (Sh Ct) 43; *Pearson v Lightning*, *Times*, 30 April 1998 CA (Civ Div); *Phee v Gordon* [2011] CSOH 181; 2011 Rep. L.R. 108 (a golfer over-confident of his ability should not have driven a ball when the claimant was in sight and might foreseeably be struck if he played a poor shot). Golf in Australia has its own special hazards: see R. Mulheron, "Golf, kangaroos and negligence 'down under'" (2000) 144 S.J. 494, commenting on *Shorten v Grafton District Golf Club Ltd* unreported 23 March 2000 NSWCA (small boy not warned of danger from kangaroos feeding in the rough of a golf course where he was searching for his ball).

[71] *Orchard v Lee* [2009] P.I.Q.R. P16; R. Weir, "Child's play" 159 N.L.J. 729.

[72] *Spry v Plowright*, *Times*, 14 March 1988 QBD.

[72a] *Tylicki v Gibbons* [2021] EWHC 3470 (QB) (although the threshold for liability was high in such a risky sport, and mere errors of judgement or lapses in skill would not be sufficient, the defendant's riding had fallen below the standard of care owed by jockeys to each other and he was therefore liable for causing the claimant's complete paraplegia).

[72b] *Tylicki v Gibbons* [2021] EWHC 3470 (QB) at [95], per HH Judge Walden-Smith.

After paragraph 8-27, add new paragraph:

8-27a When assessing breach of duty in such cases it is important to take into account the contemporaneous evidence and the decisions of the officials charged with the task of administering the rules of the game. Thus, in a claim involving an alleged "bad tackle" which ended a player's professional footballing career, it was wrong not to consider the evidence of the referee, who had a full view of the incident and had not awarded a foul.[72c] However, such evidence will not be determinative. Thus, there was liability notwithstanding a Stewards' Enquiry which concluded that there had been merely accidental interference: that conclusion had been based on insufficient evidence and limited opportunity for detailed consideration.[72d]

[72c] *Fulham Football Club v Jones* [2022] EWHC 1108 (QB).

[72d] *Tylicki v Gibbons* [2021] EWHC 3470 (QB).

(E) Other factors

Common practice

Replace footnote 129 with:

8-45 [129] *Mahon v Osborne* [1939] 2 K.B. 14 at 43, per MacKinnon LJ; *Whiteford v Hunter* [1950] W.N. 553; *Wright v CC* [1952] 2 All E.R. 789; *Simmons v Pennington & Son* [1955] 1 W.L.R. 183; *Morris v West Hartlepool Steam Navigation Co Ltd* [1956] A.C. 552; *Stokes v Guest, Keen and Nettlefold (Bolts and Nuts) Ltd* [1968] 1 W.L.R. 1776, 1783; *Henderson v H.E. Jenkins & Sons* [1969] 2 Q.B. 188 (reversed [1970] A.C. 282). *Gray v Stead* [1999] 2 Lloyd's Rep. 559, CA; Ch.12, para.12-62 (fisherman not wearing life jacket: no liability where no practice to wear one). See also *Warner v Scapa Flow Charters* [2022] CSIH 25; 2022 S.L.T. 609 (the operators of a dive boat were not liable for the death of a technical diver who fell over whilst wearing his fins on deck: at first instance the court had failed to give any weight to the fact that it was usual practice for such divers to walk a short distance to the exit point in fins).

Guidance from statutory regulation or codes

After paragraph 8-54, add new paragraph:

8-54a Medical practitioners abiding by guidelines issued by the National Institute for Clinical Excellence are likely to be acting reasonably and in discharge of their professional obligations.[161a] However, such national clinical guidelines are not a substitute for clinical judgement and departure from a national guideline does not necessarily provide prima facie evidence of negligence, although such a departure is likely to call for explanation.[161b]

[161a] See Ch.10, para.10-144; and see *Jones v Taunton and Somerset NHS Foundation Trust* [2019] EWHC 1408 (QB).

[161b] See *O'Brien v Guy's and St Thomas' NHS Trust* [2022] EWHC 2735 (KB); and *Hewes v West Herefordshire Hospitals NHS Trust* [2020] EWCA Civ 1523. See further, Ch.10, para.10-144.

Degree of skill

Replace paragraph 8-58 with:

8-58 The *Bolam* test is of general application when assessing the standard of care appropriate from someone deploying some expertise and is not confined to the particular skill of medicine.[172] Indeed the test is of universal application when assessing such professional conduct and is extremely flexible: it was used to assess whether a professional art dealer had been negligent in selling a painting by French painter Jean-Baptiste Siméon Chardin (1699–1779) as merely being a "partially autograph" work rather than "wholly autograph".[172a] The standard is that of an ordinary competent person in the same calling. He or she should do "all that any skilful person could reasonably be expected to do in such a case".[173] A person driving a car on the public highway, for example, was bound to exercise the skill of a reasonably careful driver, even before the introduction of driving tests, and, if he failed to do so, was not excused by the fact that he was using such care and skill as he possessed. The standard of care is not affected or reduced merely because the driver happens to be a learner driver, since he must comply with the same objective and impersonal standard as must every other driver.[174] In a medical context, a hospital doctor is to be judged by the standard of skill and care appropriate to the post which he or she is fulfilling. That involves leaving out of account the particular experience of the doctor or their length of service. Whether doctors are performing their normal role or "acting up", they are judged by reference to the post which they are fulfilling at the material time.[174a]

[172] *Gold v Haringey HA* [1988] Q.B. 481 at 489; [1987] 3 W.L.R. 649 CA (Civ Div), per Lloyd LJ.

[172a] *Feilding v Simon C Dickinson Ltd* [2022] EWHC 3091 (Ch); [2023] P.N.L.R. 7 (no negligence for selling the painting for £1.15 million even though when cleaned and Chardin's signature was discovered, it was re-sold for $10.5 million; nobody in the art world would have been prepared to assert that the painting was wholly autograph and, in those circumstances, the art dealer's judgement was not negligent).

[173] *Jones v Bird* 106 E.R. 1397; (1822) 5 B. & Ald. 837 KB at 845, per Bayley J.

[174] *Nettleship v Weston* [1971] 2 Q.B. 691. See further, Ch.11, para.11-281.

[174a] See *FB v Princess Alexandra Hospital NHS Trust* [2017] EWCA Civ 334; [2017] P.I.Q.R. P17 at [49], per Jackson LJ; see also see *Wilsher v Essex AHA* [1987] Q.B. 730; [1987] 2 W.L.R. 425 CA (Civ Div). For a recent application of this principle, see *CDE v Surrey and Sussex Healthcare NHS Trust* [2022] EWHC 2590 (KB).

Deciding the standard of care

Replace paragraph 8-63 with:

It is for the judge at first instance to determine what, in all the circumstances of the case, is a reasonable standard of care.[180] An appellate court will not interfere with such a determination, unless it can be demonstrated that the judge had erred.[181] In coming to a decision the overwhelming probability is that the trial judge will have regard to one, frequently more than one, of the general matters set out above. No doubt the weight to be attached to a particular circumstance will depend upon the evidence. But it will also depend upon the approach in similar circumstances taken in earlier cases. Expert evidence will often be relied upon in attempting to establish the applicable standard of care in any given case. Such expert evidence is increasingly to be found in the reports of single jointly instructed experts;[182] unless issues such as complexity and/or proportionality would permit both parties to instruct their own expert of choice. Although an uncontroverted expert's report is not bound to be accepted by the court, and may be challenged even though no positive contrary expert evidence has been adduced, if that expert opinion is logical it may be difficult to successfully challenge short of it amounting to a bare *ipse dixit*.[183] The chapters that follow seek to illustrate the standard of care that has been regarded as appropriate in the various general areas to which their heading refers. 8-63

[180] *Haley v LEB* [1965] A.C. 778. But cf. *Pritchard v Post Office* [1950] W.N. 310 where the blind claimant's own negligence was held to have been the cause of his accident. See further para.8-19.

[181] *Kite v Nolan* [1983] R.T.R. 253 (the minor claimant, aged five, ran out into the road from a line of parked cars, in order to get to an ice-cream van that was parked on the opposite side of the road. The defendant was driving his car along the road slowly, at about 15mph but could not stop in time to avoid striking the child. It was held that, as the accident could have been avoided only if the defendant had been travelling at a crawling speed of around 5mph, no negligence had been established against him and the CA declined to interfere with such a finding).

[182] See CPR Pt 35.7, Sweet & Maxwell, *The White Book* (2023) in relation to the court's power to direct that evidence is to be given by a single joint expert.

[183] *Griffiths v TUI (UK) Ltd* [2021] EWCA Civ 1442; [2022] P.I.Q.R. P5. See also *Woolley v Essex CC* [2006] EWCA Civ 753 (the court must analyse an expert's report rather than accepting it at face value); see also *White v Secretary of State for Health and Social Care* [2022] EWHC 3082 (KB) (which demonstrates the dangers of a party failing to adduce its own expert evidence and simply attempting to impugn that adduced by the other side).

CHAPTER 9

DANGEROUS PREMISES

TABLE OF CONTENTS

4. THE DUTY OWED

(A) The common duty of care

Illustrations of no liability

Replace footnote 169 with:

[169] *Cockerill v CXK Ltd* [2018] EWHC 1155 (QB). See also *Juj v John Lewis Partnership Plc* [2022] EWHC 2418 (KB); [2023] R.T.R. 8 where a kerb in a supermarket car park did not create sufficient risk of injury to trigger s.1(1) of the 1957 Act. Though as to the approach to obvious risks now see *White Lion Hotel v James* [2021] EWCA Civ 31, discussed at para.9-13 and following. **9-41**

(D) Duty to those engaged in work

ILLUSTRATIONS

Replace paragraph 9-66 with:

9-66 On the other hand, an occupier was not liable where an experienced and skilled window-cleaner fell from a height, having lost balance when some ornamental trellis-work broke away;[271] where a clerk of works fell from a scaffold, not itself defective, there being no risk other than that ordinarily incident to the use of any scaffold;[272] where an occupier had failed to design his premises in such a way that, in the event of a fire, it would be safe for the firemen, who were attending the scene of the blaze;[273] where two chimney-sweeps died by carbon monoxide poisoning, whilst they were engaged in sealing up a sweep-hole in a flue, which led from the occupier's boiler room;[274] where a farmer left a trailer on the road by his property to which cattle feed was to be delivered and while straddling a gap between the trailer and his own vehicle a delivery man fell and was injured;[275] where the lid of a skip into which a cleaner was emptying rubbish blew shut, injuring him, the occupiers of the premises where he was working were entitled to expect that his employers, who were on notice of the danger, had assessed the risk to their staff and provided accordingly;[276] where an experienced roofing contractor fell through a fragile roof when he lost his balance whilst wrestling with a length of guttering and so stepped off a crawling board.[276a]

[271] *Caddis v Gettrup* (1967) 202 E.G. 517.

[272] *Howitt v Alfred Bagnall & Sons* [1967] 2 Lloyd's Rep. 370 QBD.

[273] *Sibbald v Sher Bros, Times,* 1 February 1980 HL, although cf. *Hartley v British Railways Board* (1981) 125 S.J. 169 CA (Civ Div).

[274] *Roles v Nathan* [1963] 1 W.L.R. 1117 CA at 1123–1124, per Lord Denning MR: "The occupier here was under no duty of care to these sweeps, at any rate in regard to the dangers which caused their deaths. If it had been a different danger, as for instance if the stairs leading to the cellar gave way, the occupier might no doubt be responsible, but not for these dangers which were special risks ordinarily incidental to their calling."

[275] *Phillips v Perry* unreported 6 March 1997 CA (Civ Div).

[276] *Hannington v Mitie Cleaning (South East) Ltd* [2002] EWCA Civ 1847.

[276a] *Lewin v Gray* [2023] EWHC 112 (KB).

(G) Effect of contract

ILLUSTRATIONS

Replace footnote 352 with:

9-103 [352] *Hall v Brooklands Auto-Racing Club* [1933] 1 K.B. 205; *Wilks v Cheltenham Homeguard Motor Cycle and Light Car Club* [1971] 1 W.L.R. 668 (a motorcycle scramble race where the CA allowed the competing rider's appeal). See also *White v Blackmore* [1972] 2 Q.B. 651. In *Eaton v The Auto-Cycle Union Ltd (t/a ACU)* [2022] EWHC 2642 (KB), the claimant was seriously injured in a motorcycle race but failed to establish that the defendant organisers were at fault for not deploying straw bales in addition to tyres by way of a crash barrier, on the grounds that the prevailing guidance favoured tyres alone and the deployment of straw bales would have made the circuit more and not less dangerous. The claimant succeeded in establishing that the organisers were in breach of duty in failing to tie the tyres together but following *South Australia Asset Management Corp v York Montague Ltd* [1997] A.C. 191; [1996] P.N.L.R. 455 the court concluded that whilst this amounted to a breach of duty as it contravened the terms of the organisers licence, the scope of the duty was directed towards the elimination of the risk that tyres would come onto the track and that the claimant's accident would have occurred whether the tyres were tied together or not. His claim was therefore dismissed.

6. LIABILITY OF VENDORS, LESSORS, BUILDERS AND LOCAL AUTHORITIES

(B) Statutory liability

The Defective Premises Act 1972

(i) Duty to build dwellings properly

After paragraph 9-150, add new paragraph:

The scope of the 1972 Act has been significantly widened by the Building Safety Act 2022. This Act is long, complex and very wide-ranging[505a] and a full analysis is outside the scope of this work, but in relation to dangerous premises the Act introduces a new s.2A which provides that the duties imposed by s.1(1) of the Defective Premises Act 1972 are also owed by any person who, in the course of a business "takes on work in relation to any part of a relevant building" to the person for whom the work is done and to each person who acquires an interest (whether legal or equitable) in a dwelling in the building. The scope of the 1972 Act is therefore widened to include refurbishment and extension works as well as widening the class of duty holders. Section 2A came into force from 28th June 2022 and s.1(1) remains in force in addition to it. Significant changes are made to the limitation period applicable to actions under ss.1 and 2A of the 1972 Act.[505b] In addition, the 2022 Act also contains provisions for implementing s.38 of the Building Act 1984 by providing that personal injury or property damage caused by breach of the building regulations (in force as at the time of construction) will now be actionable subject to provisions to the contrary, though this section has not yet come into force. **9-150a**

[505a] See for example the provisions for a regulatory regime for higher risk buildings and the extensive provisions for regulations concerning construction products and cladding introduced in response to the Grenfell Tower disaster.

[505b] See para.9-165.

Replace footnote 508 with:

[508] In *Lessees and Management Co of Herons Court v Heronslea Ltd* [2019] EWCA Civ 1423; [2020] H.L.R. 11, the "provision of a dwelling house" was interpreted as involving positive steps contributing to the creation of the dwelling. The section therefore applies to architects and engineers who prescribe how the dwelling is to be created, not just to those who physically create it. It does not, however, extend to those whose role is the essentially negative one of seeing that no work is done which contravenes building regulations, such as an approved building inspector. However, see now s.2A of the 1972 Act. **9-151**

Replace footnote 511 with:

[511] *Jenson v Faux* [2011] EWCA Civ 423; [2011] 2 P. & C.R. 11, where it was pointed out that it had been decided in *Saigol v Cranley Mansions Ltd* unreported 6 July 1995 CA (Civ Div) (1995 CA Transcript No.658) and *Jacobs v Moreton* (1994) 72 B.L.R. 92 QBD that s.1 applied to the creation of a new dwelling and not to rectification of an existing dwelling but this had been overlooked in *Bayoumi v Protim Services Ltd* (1998) 30 H.L.R. 785; [1997] P.N.L.R. 189 CA (Civ Div). Both parties agreed that the court was bound by *Saigol*. However, see now s.2A of the 1972 Act. **9-152**

When a cause of action accrues

Replace paragraph 9-165 with:

The effect of these words was considered in *Alderson v Beetham Organisation* **9-165**

Ltd.[541] At the time a conversion of flats was completed in May 1994 the developer was in breach of duty in that no adequate damp proofing was provided. Work was carried out in May 1995 to rectify ensuing damp problems by relaying paving stones and providing new drainage pipes. Subsequently, a tenant suffered damage as a result of dampness and when proceedings were issued in January 2001 the developer argued that they were out of time, more than six years having elapsed since completion of the conversion work. In the result, s.1(5) was held to apply to all further work carried out to rectify the original work. It was right that the further work was not to the damp proofing, but it was dampness which had rendered the flats unfit for habitation and a fresh cause of action arose where the later work did not rectify the original work as intended. The importance of *Alderson* is much reduced by the effect of s.135 of the Building Safety Act 2022 which amends the Limitation Act 1980 by introducing a new s.4B which applies to actions under ss.1 and 2A of the Defective Premises Act 1972 (and will apply to actions under s.38 of the Building Act 1984 when it comes into force) by introducing a limitation period of 15 years from the date on which the cause of action accrues instead of the present six-year period. More controversially, s.135 further amends s.4B of the Limitation Act 1980 by providing for a retrospective 30-year limitation period in relation to claims under s.1 of the Defective Premises Act 1972 (though not s.2A).[541a] The potentially very considerable effect of this provision on claims long thought to be time-barred is circumscribed by s.135(5) which provides that where a claim would formerly have been time-barred, it will nevertheless be dismissed if it is necessary to do so to avoid a breach of the relevant defendant's convention rights as defined in the Human Rights Act 1998 (presumably largely the art.6 right to a fair trial).

[541] *Alderson v Beetham Organisation Ltd* [2003] EWCA Civ 408; [2003] H.L.R. 60. See also *Sportcity 4 Management Ltd v Countryside Properties (UK) Ltd* [2020] EWHC 1591 (TCC); [2020] 2 P. & C.R. DG21.

[541a] See now *BDW Trading Ltd v AECOM Infrastructure & Environment UK Ltd* unreported 14 December 2022 KBD (TCC) where the court allowed as arguable proposed amendments by a property developer to a claim against the defendant structural engineers relating to structural defects in high-rise residential buildings. The proposed amendments sought a contribution under the Civil Liability (Contribution) Act 1978 on the basis that the defendant was liable to the claimant under s.1 of the 1972 Act and that after s.135 of the 2022 Act both the claimant and the defendants now faced a liability to the homeowners whose properties were defective.

CHAPTER 10

PERSONS PROFESSING SOME SPECIAL SKILL

TABLE OF CONTENTS

1. ACTIONS AGAINST SKILLED PERSONS GENERALLY

(A) Introduction

The standard of care and skill

Replace footnote 15 with:

[15] *Edward Wong Finance Co v Johnson Stokes & Master* [1984] A.C. 296; [1984] 2 W.L.R. 1 PC (the Hong Kong conveyancing practice of handing over the purchase price of property to the vendor's solicitor, in advance of the date of completion, on an undertaking to keep the money safely and repay it if the contract was not completed). However, where a doctor prescribed a high dose of an antibiotic to a patient with impaired renal function and did so in the knowledge of a risk of damage to his hearing, applying the *Bolam* test he was not negligent in his judgement that the risk was justified in order to control the patient's worsening sepsis: *O'Brien v Guy's and St Thomas' NHS Trust* [2022] EWHC 2735 (KB). **10-03**

Expert evidence

Replace footnote 23 with:

10-05 [23] The duties and responsibilities of expert witnesses were summarised by Cresswell J in *National Justice Compania Naviera SA v Prudential Assurance Co Ltd (The Ikarian Reefer) (No.1)* [1993] 2 Lloyd's Rep. 68 at 81–82; [1993] F.S.R. 563 QBD (Comm) (quoted with approval in *Vernon v Bosley (No.1)* [1997] 1 All E.R. 577 at 601; [1997] R.T.R. 1 CA (Civ Div)), also *Kennedy v Cordia (Services) LLP* [2016] 1 W.L.R. 597 at [52]). For a case where care and employment experts were roundly criticised for want of independence, for acting as advocates for the claimant, for failing to assist the judge with detailed and logical analysis correlated with the evidence and for failing to respond to the radically different evidential picture of the claimant's abilities which emerged prior to and at trial, see *Muyepa v Ministry of Defence* [2022] EWHC 2648 (KB). As to the need for an expert to be independent, see *Liverpool Roman Catholic Archdiocese Trustees Inc v Goldberg (No.3)* [2001] 1 W.L.R. 2337 at 2340; [2001] 4 All E.R. 950 Ch D (a claim for professional negligence against a barrister specialising in tax matters); per Evans-Lombe J: "where it is demonstrated that there exists a relationship between the proposed expert and the party calling him which a reasonable observer might think was capable of affecting the views of the expert so as to make them unduly favourable to that party, his evidence should not be admitted however unbiased the conclusions of the expert might probably be."

Replace paragraph 10-07 with:

10-07 The duty of a court receiving evidence from experts on matters within their expertise is to examine it in a critical way to ensure it has a logical and defensible basis.[30] Where one expert opinion is preferred to another, a court should support its preference with reasons.[31] Such reasons may turn upon the court coming to a different view of the facts[32] to that taken by the witness, or upon a preference for the inherent likelihood of one view over another. The important point is that a reasoned basis for the choice must be given.[33] A variety of factors should be considered, including whether an expert opinion is tendered in good faith, whether it is reasonable and whether the expert advancing it is competent and responsible: by far the most important consideration is the logic or otherwise of the expert opinion tendered.[34] The court is not obliged to accept the uncontroverted evidence of an expert witness which complies with the formal requirements of CPR Pt 35. Such evidence falls to be evaluated and assessed and its weight, if any will depend on the circumstances of the case, the nature of the report and the purpose for which it is adduced.[34a] In an appropriate case the court may receive expert evidence even if, in breach of the Code of Guidance on Expert Evidence annexed to the Civil Procedure Rules, most of the expert's work has been carried out on a contingency fee basis: one solution is to receive the evidence but assess the risk of bias in the light of cross examination.[35]

[30] See Lord Browne-Wilkinson's observations about the *Bolam* test in *Bolitho v City and Hackney HA* [1998] A.C. 232 at 240, 241; [1998] P.I.Q.R. P10 HL. See further, R. Heywood, "The logic of Bolitho" (2006) 22(4) P.N. 225. It will be a heavy burden to show that a decision, supported by a body of professional opinion, was nonetheless unreasonable. Save in cases of stark illogicality it will normally require expert evidence to undermine that body of opinion: see *Williams v CWM TAF Local Health Board* [2018] EWCA Civ 1745, see also para.10-137.

[31] See, e.g. *Flannery v Halifax Estate Agencies Ltd* [2000] 1 W.L.R. 377; [2000] C.P. Rep. 18 CA (Civ Div); also *Smith v Southampton University Hospital NHS Trust* [2007] EWCA Civ 387 (a clinical negligence claim in which there was an issue between expert witnesses whether surgery had been carried out negligently and, in rejecting a particular allegation the judge said only that the expert relied upon by the defendant was highly reputable and that it had not been suggested that he did not represent the view of a responsible body of relevant medical opinion); also *Smith v Hammond* [2010] EWCA Civ 725; [2010] R.T.R. 30 (in a road traffic accident case a judge was not entitled to reject expert evidence because it did not accord with his own experience).

[32] For an example where it was permissible to reject the views of competent experts, genuinely held, about what was ultimately a question of fact, see *Penney v East Kent HA* [2000] P.N.L.R. 323 CA (Civ Div), para.10-180. See in relation to medical experts, para.10-137.

[33] For a case in which the court was entitled to reject expert opinion see *Marriott v West Midlands Regional RHA* [1999] Lloyd's Rep. Med. 23 CA (Civ Div) (claimant's GP negligent in failing to refer him to hospital after head injury even though an expert witness had said that keeping him at home under review was a reasonable course of action); also *D v South Tyneside Health Care NHS Trust* [2003] EWCA Civ 878; [2004] P.I.Q.R. P12 (a dispute between experts about the appropriate intervals between which a patient, detained in hospital in her own interests pursuant to the Mental Health Act 1983, should have been kept under observation). But in *Calver v Westwood Veterinary Group* [2001] P.I.Q.R. P11 CA (Civ Div) it was not permissible to prefer one body of veterinary opinion to another where there was nothing in the evidence to allow the conclusion that the opinion of the expert relied upon by the defendant was illogical (an allegation of negligent treatment of a horse after it had aborted a foal).

[34] See *Jones v Taunton and Somerset NHS Foundation Trust* [2019] EWHC 1408 (QB); [2019] Med. L.R. 384. See also para.10-138. In *Gulf View Medical Centre Ltd v Tesheira* [2022] UKPC 38, the Privy Council considered that it did not matter that experts were not familiar with the *Bolam* test. They were medical experts not legal experts and it was their medical evidence which fell to be evaluated.

[34a] *Griffiths v TUI (UK) Ltd* [2021] EWCA Civ 1442; [2022] P.I.Q.R. P5, though any departure from properly reasoned opinion on matters within the expertise of such a witnesses will require cogent explanation, see *White v Secretary of State for Health and Social Care* [2022] EWHC 3082 (KB).

[35] *Davis v Stena Line Ltd* [2005] EWHC 420 (QB); [2005] 2 Lloyd's Rep. 13. In a clinical negligence claim, a medical expert relied upon by the defendant was not automatically disqualified because he had been at a time before the trial a member of the cases committee of the Medical Defence Union. It was observed that when an expert provided a report he should produce his CV, which should include details of any employment or activity which raised a possible conflict of interest: *Toth v Jarman* [2006] EWCA Civ 1028; [2006] C.P. Rep. 44. See Iller, "Conflicted experts" 2006 P.I.L.J. 50, 23.

Delegation of task

Replace footnote 59 with:

[59] *Barclays Bank Plc v Various Claimants* [2020] UKSC 13; [2020] P.I.Q.R. P11 and see Ch.7, para.7-45. For a case in which the owner of a dental practice was held to owe a non-delegable duty of care to a patient for negligent treatment provided at his practice by both self-employed dentists and an employed dentist, see *Hughes v Rattan* [2022] EWCA Civ 107; [2022] P.I.Q.R. P11. **10-10**

The burden and standard of proof

Replace footnote 61 with:

[61] In *Dwyer v Rodrick* (1983) 80 L.S.G. 3003 CA (Civ Div), the CA observed that, whilst there are no special rules about the burden or standard of proof in cases involving professional negligence, in reality it will be harder to prove a case on the balance of probabilities where it concerns the complicated and sophisticated professional activities of, say, a medical practitioner. In *Harrington v Essex AHA Times*, 14 November 1984 QBD, the claimant failed to discharge the burden of proof in a case of clinical negligence, where there were two possible explanations for the occurrence of complications in his post-operative condition and the court was not prepared to select one of them. Likewise, *Collyer v Mid Essex Hospital Services NHS Trust* [2019] EWHC 3577 (QB), where the claimant alleged that the almost complete paralysis of his tongue must have been been caused by one of four negligent mechanisms as there was no other plausible explanation: the claim failed because, following *Rhesa Shipping Co SA v Edmunds (The Popi M)* [1985] 1 W.L.R. 948; [1985] 2 All E.R. 712 HL, none of the four mechanisms satisfied the balance of probabilities test. See also *Johnson v Williams* [2022] EWHC 1585 (QB) and Ch.13, para.13-85. See generally as to the burden and standard of proof, Ch.6, paras 6-01 to 6-07. See also Ch.6, paras 6-15 to 6-21 in relation to proof by inference. **10-11**

The duty formulae

Replace footnote 89 with:

10-21 [89] *Steel v NRAM Plc* [2018] UKSC 13; [2018] 1 W.L.R. 1190. In *McDonnell v Dass Legal Solutions (MK) Law Ltd (t/a DLS Law)* [2022] EWHC 991 (QB); [2022] Costs L.R. 855, the claimant alleged that having introduced the defendant solicitors to a client company in which he held a 70% beneficial interest though no position or shares, the solicitors were in breach of a duty owed to him to protect his interests so that when on the instructions of its sole director the client company did not complete a property purchase, the claimant was deprived of an opportunity of benefitting from the sale proceeds. The court held that there was no express retainer as between the defendant and the claimant, and that the test of necessity was not met for the purposes of establishing an implied retainer. Further, following *Steel* there was no duty of care owed to the claimant in tort as the defendant should not reasonably have foreseen that the claimant would rely on it to protect his interests.

4. AUCTIONEERS

The duty of care

Replace footnote 310 with:

10-80 [310] *Thwaytes v Sotheby's* [2015] EWHC 36 (Ch); [2015] P.N.L.R. 12 (defendant not negligent in failing to identify a painting, sold at auction for £42,000, as a Caravaggio worth many millions). In *Feilding v Simon C Dickinson Ltd* [2022] EWHC 3091 (Ch); [2023] P.N.L.R. 7, the defendant art dealer valued and sold a painting on the basis that it was not wholly by the hand of the C18th French painter Chardin. The painting was later re-sold for a substantially greater sum but the court declined to assess the conduct of the defendant by reference to the extended duty of disclosure in Montgomery and applied the *Bolam* test to conclude that he was not negligent and was under no duty to discuss with the claimants the theoretical possibility of other experts holding alternative views.

5. BANKERS AND FINANCE COMPANIES

Giving advice or information

Replace paragraph 10-86 with:

10-86 Whilst it is no part of a banker's ordinary business to give a customer advice as to investments,[317] if advice is given, an obligation may be imposed to take reasonable care.[318] When a bank chooses to give preliminary advice to a customer about the nature and effect of a proposed mortgage in the bank's favour, it is under a duty not to misstate the effect of the mortgage. Further, the bank ought to explain to its customer, where that was the case, that a mortgage on a property, jointly owned by the customer and spouse, specifically covered additional unlimited advances to the spouse.[319] A duty of care was owed where a bank manager was asked for and gave advice about the wisdom of purchasing a particular house as a business venture.[320] A duty to provide information will be easier to infer if the bank has signed up to adhere to protocols which require the giving of information in particular situations, such as the Business Banking Code.[321]

[317] See also *Lipkin Gorman v Karpnale Ltd* [1989] 1 W.L.R. 1340 CA (Civ Div) (a bank's principal duty is to pay cheques signed in accordance with its mandate and there is no obligation imposed on it to inquire into the commercial wisdom of any transaction. A bank would be liable in such circumstances only if, on the facts found, any reasonable banker would have suspected fraud). In *Taylor v Legal and General Partnership Services Ltd* [2022] EWHC 2475 (Ch); [2023] P.N.L.R. 4, the court held that whilst mortgage brokers arranging finance owed a borrower a duty to take reasonable care to provide accurate information and to obtain full relevant information, this did not extend to advising on the financial prudence of the transaction or to advising on the need for independent financial advice.

[318] *Woods v Martins Bank Ltd* [1959] 1 Q.B. 55 at 72 (see para.10-87), per Salmon J. See also *Denning v Greenhalgh Financial Services Ltd* [2017] EWHC 143 QB; [2017] P.N.L.R. 19 (the most

important consideration governing the scope of a professional's duty is the retainer: for an extended duty to arise there must to be a close factual and legal nexus between the retainer and the matter in relation to which it is alleged the professional has omitted to advise).

[319] *Cornish v Midland Bank Plc* [1985] 3 All E.R. 513 CA (Civ Div).

[320] *Verity v Lloyds Bank Plc* [1995] C.L.C. 1557; [1995] N.P.C. 148 QBD.

[321] *Thomas v Triodos Bank NV* [2017] EWHC 314 (QB); [2017] 1 C.L.C. 536 (a bank which had signed up to the Business Banking Code thereby owed a duty provide information on the implications of fixing interest rates on a loan, although the duty arose only in response to a client's request).

The standard of care

Replace footnote 354 with:

[354] *Barclays Bank v Quincecare Ltd and Unichem Ltd* [1992] 4 All E.R. 363 QBD (Comm). Contrast *Singularis Holdings Ltd (In Liquidation) v Daiwa Capital Markets Europe Ltd* [2019] UKSC 50; [2020] P.N.L.R. 5, where a bank was liable even though payments were made to third parties from the company's account as a result of a director's fraud, see para.10-31. The court in *Nigeria v JP Morgan Chase Bank NA* [2022] EWHC 1447 (Comm) stressed that in order to establish breach of a bank's *Quincecare* duty it was necessary to establish "gross negligence" in the sense of an obvious risk of fraud coupled with a serious disregard for that risk. As to "gross negligence" see further Ch.1, para.1-15. In *Royal Bank of Scotland International Ltd v JP SPC 4* [2022] UKPC 18; [2022] P.N.L.R. 22, the Privy Council conducted a thorough review of the authorities and was at pains to stress that the duty identified in *Quincecare* was owed only to the bank's customer and did not extend to third parties such as the beneficial owner of money held in the customer's account. To the extent that it held otherwise, the case of *Baden v Société Générale pour Favouriser le Développement du Commerce et d'Industrie en France SA* [1993] 1 W.L.R. 509 Ch D was wrongly decided as having been arrived at by reference to the now discredited test for the existence of a duty of care propounded by Lord Wilberforce in *Anns v Merton LBC* [1978] A.C. 728; [1977] 2 W.L.R. 1024 HL. **10-100**

6. Barristers

The duty of care

Replace footnote 384 with:

[384] See *Robinson v Chief Constable of West Yorkshire Police* [2018] UKSC 4; [2018] P.I.Q.R. P9 at [29], per Lord Reed. See paras 10-19 to 10-24. For a first instance decision in which a barrister was held to owe a duty of care to a third party, see *Mathew v Maughold Life Assurance Co Ltd* (1985) 1 P.N. 142 (the case went to appeal, see [1995] P.N.L.R. 51, but the existence of such a duty was not in issue by that stage). See also *McClean v Thornhill* [2022] EWHC 457 (Ch), where a barrister who provided advice to the promoters of a tax avoidance scheme did not owe a duty to subscribers to the scheme in circumstances where it was expressly stipulated that they should take independent advice and that they should warrant that they had obtained and relied on such advice. **10-107**

7. Dentists

The duty of care

Replace footnote 427 with:

[427] *Hughes v Rattan* [2022] EWCA Civ 107; [2022] P.I.Q.R. P11: on the basis of the criteria set out in *Woodland v Swimming Teachers Association* [2013] UKSC 66; [2014] A.C. 537 (see Ch.7, paras 7-106 to 7-120), a dentist's duty to a patient was held to include a non-delegable duty in respect of treatment received from self-employed associate dentists to whom he had granted a non-exclusive licence to practice from his premises pursuant to the British Dental Association's standard model. It was decided *obiter dictum* that he was not vicariously liable for the tortious acts or omissions of the associate dentists. **10-116**

8. MEDICAL PRACTITIONERS

Setting the standard of care

Replace footnote 519 with:

10-147 [519] *FB v Princess Alexandra Hospital NHS Trust* [2017] EWCA Civ 334; [2017] P.I.Q.R. P17 (a senior house officer working in A&E failed to ask parents what symptoms led to their bringing their child into hospital at 4.00am: the suggestion that it was not negligent for such a doctor to fail to ask for a proper history was rejected, history-taking being a basic skill which hospital doctors at every level were expected to possess). See also *Andrews v Greater Glasgow Health Board* [2019] CSOH 31; 2019 S.L.T. 727.

ILLUSTRATIONS

Replace footnote 607 with:

10-163 [607] *Joyce v Merton, Sutton and Wandsworth HA* (1996) 27 B.M.L.R. 124. See also *CDE v Surrey and Sussex Healthcare NHS Trust* [2022] EWHC 2590 (KB), where the claimant failed to prove that she would not have developed cerebral palsy had a caesarian section been carried out earlier.

Failure to warn of risks

Replace footnote 615 with:

10-165 [615] *Smith v Barking, Havering and Brentwood HA* [1994] 5 Med. L. Rev. 285 (claimant facing likely onset of tetraplegia in nine months elected to have an operation which was attended with risk of immediate onset of the same condition. She was not warned of the risk. Her claim failed on a finding that even if she had been so informed she would have given consent: per Hutchinson J, at 288–289, while the question has to be decided on a subjective basis: "If everything points to the fact that a reasonable claimant properly informed, would have assented to the operation, the assertion from the witness box, made after the adverse outcome is known, in a wholly artificial situation and in the knowledge that the outcome of the case depends on that assertion being maintained, does not carry great weight unless there are extraneous or additional factors to substantiate it." Similar observations were made in *Webb v Barclays Bank Plc*; sub nom. *Webb v Portsmouth Hospitals NHS Trust* [2001] EWCA Civ 1141; [2002] P.I.Q.R. P8 (the Court of Appeal disagreed with the suggestion that where the basis of claim is failure to inform, the claimant must give evidence as to what would or would not have happened had the relevant information been given. By the date of trial it may well be difficult to attach particular weight to the claimant's own evidence on the question, conditioned as it must be by complex emotions reflecting, for instance, the legal proceedings themselves, as well as the extent to which the claimant perceives the procedure in issue to have been successful or not and has adapted to resulting disability). In *Watts v North Bristol NHS Trust* [2022] EWHC 2048 (QB), the claimant's spinal fusion surgery did not produce the hoped-for outcome and he alleged that the possibility of microdiscectomy had not been canvassed with him. The court concluded that the two operations were directed towards different ends and reiterated that whilst the claimant was under a burden to prove that he would have chosen microdiscectomy had he been properly informed, his own ex post fact assertion as to what he would have done carried much less weight than the surrounding objective evidence.

The scope of the duty

After "the defendant's negligence."", add new footnote 632a:

10-170 [632a] In *D v Grampian Health Board* [2022] CSOH 63, the court concluded obiter dictum and applying the test in *Khan* that had midwives been culpable in failing to transfer the pregnant pursuer from the antenatal ward to the labour ward, the scope of their duty did not extend to responsibility for the acts or omissions of different medical professionals on the labour ward.

9. HOSPITALS AND HEALTH AUTHORITIES

The standard of care

Replace footnote 659 with:

[659] *Wilsher v Essex AHA* [1987] Q.B. 730; [1987] 2 W.L.R. 425 CA (Civ Div) (appeal allowed on the issue of causation [1988] A.C. 1074; [1988] 2 W.L.R. 557 HL). For the standard of care generally, para.10-03. Also *Andrews v Greater Glasgow Health Board* [2019] CSOH 31; 2019 S.L.T. 727 where the court held that a junior doctor was to be held to the standards applicable to his post and could not discharge his duty of care by relying on a more senior doctor. See further para.10-03. **10-179**

ILLUSTRATIONS

Replace footnote 668 with:

[668] *Lepine v University Hospital Board* (1964) 50 D.L.R. (2d) 225, affirmed (1965) 54 D.L.R. (2d) 340. Likewise, in *Selfe v Ilford and District Hospital Management Committee* (1970) 114 S.J. 935, the hospital was guilty of negligence in failing to provide continuous supervision of a psychiatric patient and a known suicide risk, who left his bed by a ground floor window, climbed to a roof and threw himself off. See also *G's Curator Bonis v Grampian Health Board*, 1995 S.L.T. 652, where the hospital was liable to the claimant, a known suicide risk on "close observation", who was found hanging from a shower fitment; also *Webley v St George's Hospital NHS Trust* [2014] EWHC 299 (QB); (2014) 138 B.M.L.R. 190, Bean J (failure by security guards to cover the side door in a cubicle thereby permitting a mentally ill patient from running outside, where he fell down a 15ft drop and was injured). See also *Paterson v Lanarkshire Health Board* [2023] CSOH 1; 2023 S.L.T. 67, where the health board was negligent for failing to arrange for suitable follow-up appointments for a mentally ill patient who committed suicide shortly after discharge in circumstances where suicide was one of a reasonably foreseeable range of damaging outcomes. **10-180**

Replace footnote 677 with:

[677] *Caparo Industries Plc v Dickman* [1990] 2 A.C. 605. See Jones, "Liabilities for psychiatric patients: setting the boundaries" (2000) 1 P.N. 3. See also *Traylor v Kent and Medway NHS Social Care Partnership Trust* [2022] EWHC 260 (QB); [2022] P.I.Q.R. P12 where the defendant was not liable to the claimant who, suffering from paranoid schizophrenia, stabbed his daughter several times and was shot and seriously injured by the police as a result. On the facts, the defendant had taken reasonable steps to avoid the risk that the claimant would suffer from a relapse. His daughter's claim under the Human Rights Act 1998 was also dismissed on the grounds that the defendant had taken reasonable steps to address and was not in breach of her convention rights. See further, Ch.4, para.4-287a. **10-183**

14. SOLICITORS

(A) The duty of care

Contractual duty to client

After "engaged to act.", add new footnote 899a:

[899a] A retainer is not created by responding to a solicitor's television advertisement, even when the potential client corresponded and received some advice thereafter. The advertisement was at best an invitation to treat, there was no implied retainer as the solicitor's conduct was consistent with its seeking information to decide whether to offer to enter into a retainer and there was no tortious duty of care arising out of the limited and generic information provided by the solicitor. Accordingly, the claimant failed to establish liability against the solicitors for not advising her to notify a travel agency of her claim for serious personal injuries, with the result that insurers declined cover on their eventually being notified: *Miller v Irwin Mitchell LLP* [2022] EWHC 2252 (Ch); [2023] P.N.L.R. 1. **10-239**

Illustrations

Replace footnote 943 with:

10-249 [943] See paras 10-19 to 10-23, and *Ashraf v Lester Dominic Solicitors* [2023] EWCA Civ 4 where the court refused summary judgment on the basis that it was arguable that a solicitor had stepped outside his retainer and acted for all parties to a property transaction, thereby assuming a responsibility to non-clients.

(B) The standard of care

Time-limit for action against negligent solicitor

Replace footnote 1240 with:

10-306 [1240] *Khan v RM Falvey & Co* [2002] EWCA Civ 400; [2002] P.N.L.R. 28. This result cannot generally be avoided by suggesting that there is a continuing duty on a lawyer to review their previous advice: see *Sciortino v Beaumont* [2021] EWCA Civ 786; [2021] Ch. 365 at [50], per Coulson LJ and *Capita (Banstead 2011) Ltd v RFIB Group Ltd* [2015] EWCA Civ 1310; [2016] P.N.L.R. 17. *Capita* was followed in *PSGS Trust Corp Ltd v Aon UK Ltd* [2022] EWHC 2058 (Ch); [2023] P.N.L.R. 2 where the court struck out those of the claimant's allegations which asserted a continuing duty on the part of advisors to re-visit their advice until the end of their retainer. The cause of action crystallised when the claimant acted on their advice. For a case in which it was held that a continuing duty was owed in contract and tort so as to defeat a limitation defence, albeit in a very different context, see *Equitas Ltd v Walsham Brothers & Co Ltd* [2013] EWHC 3264 (Comm); [2014] P.N.L.R. 8.

(C) Causation and damage

Negligence in the course of a contentious case

Replace footnote 1300 with:

10-325 [1300] See, for example, *Kingsley Napley LLP v Harris* [2021] EWHC 901 (QB) (where a claim for a lost opportunity to achieve a better outcome in a solicitor's negligence action arising out of a negligence claim against another set of solicitors failed as the court held that the latter solicitors would not have made a better offer and the claimant would not have run the claim to trial). In *Coote v Ullstein* [2022] EWHC 607 (QB), the court considered that a rule of thumb had developed to the effect that prospects of success of less than 10% were insufficiently substantial to sound in damages.

Chapter 11

HIGHWAYS AND TRANSPORT

Table of Contents

1. Highways

(A) Maintenance of the highway

The Highways Act 1980

Replace footnote 14 with:

[14] *Griffiths v Liverpool Corp* [1967] 1 Q.B. 374; [1966] 3 W.L.R. 467 CA. In *Hoyle v Hampshire CC* [2022] EWHC 934 (QB), a tree adjoining the highway was not part of the fabric of the highway and the claim pursuant to s.41(1) was misconceived. **11-04**

(B) Dangers on the highway

Trees and shrubs

After "of a bus.[88]", add:

In contrast, a local authority was not liable for a fatal accident that occurred when **11-24** a tree growing by the roadside fell onto a car: the tree had been adequately inspected in monthly "drive by" inspections by highways inspectors and periodic "on foot" inspections by arboriculturists, in accordance with government guidance.[88a]

[88a] *Hoyle v Hampshire CC* [2022] EWHC 934 (QB) at [133], in which HH Judge Brimelow, albeit *obiter*

dictum, concluded that the claim pursuant to s.41 of the Highways Act 1980 was misconceived given that the tree was not part of the fabric of the highway and in any event its failure was not due to any lack of maintenance.

2. CARRIERS

(D) Ships

Safety on board

Replace paragraph 11-173 with:

11-173 In *Warner v Scapa Flow Charters*,[495] a diver on board a recreational dive boat tripped on his fins whilst walking from his seat to the dive gate. He suffered an abdominal injury but went on to dive, during which he got into difficulty and subsequently died. There was no defect in the dive vessel. Whereas at first instance the court found that the vessel's owners should have taken measures to eliminate or minimise the practice of divers walking with their fins on deck, on appeal it was held that this was setting the standard of care too high and no breach of art.3(1) was established. The deceased, who was himself a technical diver, knew the inherent risk of falling when walking in fins and it was sufficient for the operators to have provided a safe means of moving from the seat to the exit point in the form of a non-slip and unobstructed deck, handrails and a deckhand, which the deceased, as the skilled and experienced person, had chosen not to use.[495a]

[495] *Warner v Scapa Flow Charters* [2022] CSIH 25; 2022 S.L.T. 609.

[495a] *Warner v Scapa Flow Charters* [2022] CSIH 25 at [50], per Lord Carloway. In setting the standard of care, the court considered the guidance provided by cases such as *Tomlinson v Congleton BC* [2003] UKHL 47; [2004] P.I.Q.R. P8 and *White Lion Hotel (A Partnership) v James* [2021] EWCA Civ 31; [2021] P.I.Q.R. P11 in relation to engaging in activities with known and obvious risk.

(E) Aircraft

(iii) Carriage by Air Conventions

Limitation of liability

After "servants or agents;", add new footnote 549a:

11-194 [549a] In *Mather v easyJet Airline Co Ltd* [2022] CSOH 40; 2022 S.L.T. 631, an airline failed to prove that injuries sustained by a passenger, when he fell from an airport wheelchair that was being pushed by an employee of an independent contractor to the airport, when disembarking from an aircraft, were not due to its own negligence or other wrongful act or omission or that of its servants or agents, and in terms of art.21(2)(a), it was liable to make reparation to him, without limit of liability. The contractor had to be regarded as the airline's agent within the meaning of art.17; the services provided were in furtherance of the contract of carriage by assisting the claimant to disembark the flight; they were also services which the airline would itself have been required by law to provide had the contractor not done so as they were part of the process of disembarkation.

3. HIGHWAY USERS AND COLLISIONS

The duty of care generally

Replace paragraph 11-205 with:

11-205 Care must be exercised when balancing the relative weight to attach to expert evidence relating to the theoretical reconstruction of road traffic accidents, as against the evidence of primary witnesses of fact:

> "[It] is the primary factual evidence which is of the greatest importance in a case of this kind. The expert evidence comprises a useful way in which that factual evidence, and the inferences to be drawn from it, can be tested. It is, however, very important to ensure that the expert evidence is not elevated into a fixed framework or formula, against which the defendant's actions are then taken to be rigidly judged with a mathematical precision."[590]

That approach was endorsed and applied by the Court of Appeal in *Taylor v Raspin*[590a] in which William Davis LJ, in agreeing with that proposition and relating to the facts of the case stated that:

> "In this case the expert evidence was of significance in providing evidence of the speed of the motorcycle though it seems to me that the judge did fall into the trap of engaging in an exercise of mathematical precision. The expert evidence was not central to the case. The lay evidence which established that the defendant pulled out of a minor road and continued to pull out even when the motorcycle was in view and when she could have stopped was paramount."[590b]

[590] *Stewart v Glaze* [2009] EWHC 704 (QB).

[590a] *Taylor v Raspin* [2022] EWCA Civ 1613; [2023] P.I.Q.R. P8.

[590b] *Taylor v Raspin* [2022] EWCA Civ 1613 at [35], per William Davis LJ.

Each decision turns on its facts

Replace paragraph 11-210 with:

It is essential always to bear in mind, when considering the text that follows, that each decision turns upon its own individual facts[599] and should be treated as a guide, rather than as a binding authority for a rule of law: **11-210**

> "The task for the court is not to reach a conclusion based on 'certainty' as to what occurred but rather to come to a reasoned view as to the most probable explanation. In many accidents there will be a range of confounding factors which render the task of *precise* reconstruction of events impossible..."
>
> "A court attempts to reconstruct the most probable answers to the core questions by applying established forensic tools to such evidence as is available. It looks at the evidence in its totality, it seeks to understand the relevant layout of the scene, identify any objective facts that might act as lodestars by which more subjective opinion and recollection can be tested, scrutinizes carefully the accounts of witnesses of fact and experts... and it applies to all of this a fair dose of common sense."[600]

In finding facts, the court should beware of adopting an overly analytical and scientific approach when trying to reconstruct the circumstances of an accident.[600a]

[599] *Scott v Warren* [1974] R.T.R. 104; *Foskett v Mistry* [1984] R.T.R. 1 CA (Civ Div).

[600] *Barrow v Merrett* [2021] EWHC 792 (QB) at [8] and [9], per Richard Hermer QC whose judgment was upheld and endorsed as "impeccable" by the Court of Appeal in *Barrow v Merrett* [2022] EWCA Civ 1241; [2023] R.T.R. 1. In relation to the factors to take into account when testing the recollection of witnesses of fact, see *Gestmin SGPS SA v Credit Suisse (UK) Ltd* [2013] EWHC 3560 (Comm); [2020] 1 C.L.C. 428 (accounts given at the time of an event tend to be more accurate than those provided later. Even honest witnesses might give wholly inaccurate evidence because their memory might have been subconsciously degraded, not just by time, but by a range of biases); see also *Onassis v Vergottis* [1968] 2 Lloyd's Rep. 403 HL.

[600a] See *Lambert v Clayton* [2009] EWCA Civ 237; [2010] R.T.R. 3 at [35]–[40], per Smith LJ; and *Zanatta v Metroline Travel Ltd* [2022] EWHC 1411 (QB).

After paragraph 11-210, add new paragraph:

11-210a Further, an appellate court should not interfere with findings of fact, inferences from findings of fact, or a judge's evaluation of facts, unless compelled to do so because those findings were wrong.[600b]

[600b] See *Fage UK Ltd v Chobani UK Ltd* [2014] EWCA Civ 5; [2014] E.T.M.R. 26; and *Barrow v Merrett* [2022] EWCA Civ 1241 at [89]–[104] (the judge had not approached the case in an unfair way: he had weighed the evidence conscientiously, and his conclusion was supported by detailed and transparent reasoning in an impeccable judgment. Most of the appellant's submissions were designed to show that the judge could have made different findings on the evidence, rather than to show that the findings he did make were wrong).

Speed

After "road in question,", add new footnote 657a:

11-228 [657a] The type of vehicle being driver will also have a bearing on the reasonableness of the speed. See *Parry v Johnson* [2022] EWHC 889 (QB) (tractor driver towing an unlit seeding machine that overhung the verge).

Look out

Replace footnote 690 with:

11-234 [690] *Chapman v Post Office* [1982] R.T.R. 165 CA (Civ Div); *Ehrari (A Child) v Curry* [2007] EWCA Civ 120; [2007] R.T.R. 42 (driver 30% to blame for wing mirror collision between lorry and a 13-year-old child who had stepped into the road from behind a parked car and who was there to be seen for about one second before impact); see also *Parry v Johnson* [2022] EWHC 889 (QB).

Road junctions

After paragraph 11-247, add new paragraph:

11-247a A driver emerging from a minor road and turning right onto a major road owes a continuing duty to vehicles travelling on the major road.[725a] How that duty is to be discharged depends on the circumstances of the case, and it might require the driver to look left for a second time before joining the far carriageway. Thus, there was liability when a car, turning right onto a major road, drove into collision with a motorcycle that was already present in the lane into which the car was intending to drive. Although the driver had looked right and left and then right again, it was incumbent upon her to look to her left for a second time: she was pulling out onto a road on which a regular flow of traffic was to be expected; the view to her left was affected by a bend; and the slow speed at which she pulled out increased the need to check for a second time that it was safe to continue.[725b]

[725a] *Taylor v Raspin* [2022] EWCA Civ 1613.

[725b] *Taylor v Raspin* [2022] EWCA Civ 1613 (although the driver's negligence was the primary cause of the accident, damages were reduced by 45% to take account of the motorcyclist having driven at excessive speed).

Lights

After "driver was negligent.[760]", add:

11-261 Similarly, a tractor driver towing an unlit seeding machine which overhung the grassy verge at dusk should have turned on his main beam headlights.[760a]

[760a] *Parry v Johnson* [2022] EWHC 889 (QB).

Sounding horns

Replace footnote 769 with:

[769] *Davies v Journeaux* [1975] 1 Lloyd's Rep. 483; [1976] R.T.R. 111 CA (Civ Div). See also *Zanatta v Metroline Travel Ltd* [2022] EWHC 1411 (QB) (no duty to sound a horn: a reasonable driver would not consider an ordinary pedestrian a hazard when there was no indication that they were about the step out into the road moments later without warning). **11-266**

Defective vehicle

After "being driven negligently.[777]", add:

In contrast, a car driver who had entered an emergency refuge area on a smart motorway when the engine warning light came on did not act negligently in continuing his journey when the light went off again. The reasonably careful and competent driver would not have anticipated a real risk that the car, being a modern vehicle that was properly and professionally maintained, would suffer a complete loss of all power shortly afterwards.[777a] **11-268**

[777a] *Vakharia v Bukowski* [2022] EWHC 673 (QB); [2022] R.T.R. 22 (the lorry driver who hit the rear of the vehicle causing fatal injuries to one of the passengers was therefore wholly liable for the accident).

Pedestrians

Replace paragraph 11-300 with:

Pedestrians have a right to use the highway and may walk on the carriageway of a road save that it is illegal to walk on a motorway or its slip roads except in an emergency.[860] Pedestrians can expect motorists to take reasonable care.[861] Indeed when apportioning liability between a negligent motorist and a negligent pedestrian the court will take into account the destructive disparity between the danger presented to a pedestrian by a negligent motorist and that presented to the motorist by the pedestrian.[862] As Hale LJ observed, "it is rare indeed for a pedestrian to be found more responsible than a driver unless the pedestrian has suddenly moved into the path of an oncoming vehicle."[863] Where the claimant stepped out into the road at a busy city centre junction in contravention of a red man pedestrian signal and was struck by a bus the pedestrian was held to be 50% to blame but the bus driver was negligent for failing to observe him sooner. Appropriate braking would not have prevented the collision but it would have reduced its damaging effect.[864] **11-300**

[860] Road Traffic Regulation Act 1984 s.17; Motorways Traffic (England & Wales) Regulations 1982 (SI 1982/1163).

[861] *Boss v Litton* 172 E.R. 1030; (1832) 5 Car. & P. 407.

[862] See e.g. *Eagle v Chambers (No.1)* [2003] EWCA Civ 1107; [2004] R.T.R. 9 per Hale LJ and *Bruma v Hassan* [2017] EWHC 3209 (QB).

[863] *Eagle v Chambers (No.1)* [2004] R.T.R. 9; also *Sabir v Osei-Kwabena* [2015] EWCA Civ 1213; [2016] R.T.R. 9 (a pedestrian who should have seen a car and clearly misjudged its position contributed to her accident by 25%; the car driver who was travelling at 30mph but did not see her until she was three or four metres away was principally to blame); also *Cameron v Nwankwo* [2022] CSOH 7 (pedestrian only one third to blame having placed herself in a hazardous position by choosing to cross a road at a point where there was no protection from oncoming traffic).

[864] *Rehill v Rider Holdings Ltd* [2012] EWCA Civ 628; [2013] R.T.R. 5. Similarly, in *Zanatta v Metroline Travel Ltd* [2022] EWHC 1411 (QB), had there been a finding of primary liability, then the court would have assessed contributory negligence at as much as 70% due to the claimant having moved out into the path of the defendant without warning. In *Hetherington v Blythe* [2023] EWHC 41 (KB), a driver was not negligent for striking a pedestrian who had run out into the road; affording the driver no opportunity to react to his presence in the road.

After "clothing were rejected.[865]", add:

11-301 In contrast, there was no liability when a car struck an 11-year old boy: the most probable series of events being that the claimant ran across the road, into the path of oncoming traffic, just after a vehicle had passed him from his left and obscured him from the defendant, who had no realistic opportunity of avoiding the collision.[865a]

[865a] *Barrow v Merrett* [2022] EWCA Civ 1241.

After paragraph 11-303, add new paragraph:

11-303a Pedestrians who were struck by an unlit seeding machine being towed by a tractor at dusk and which overhung the grassy verge of the country lane along which they were walking, were not negligent for stepping from the carriageway and onto the verge.[870a] To have remained in the road would have been dangerous; the majority of pedestrians would have considered it unwise to remain on the road in the path of an oncoming tractor during twilight hours in the hope that the driver would see them.

[870a] *Parry v Johnson* [2022] EWHC 889 (QB) (drivers towing dangerous, unlit equipment, which overhangs pavements and grassy verges, owe a duty to all pedestrians nearby on pavements and verges who might reasonably be affected by the overhang).

CHAPTER 12

EMPLOYMENT AT COMMON LAW

TABLE OF CONTENTS

1. COMMON LAW DUTY OF EMPLOYER

(A) Introduction

Nature of the duty

Replace footnote 10 with:

[10] Per Lord Wright, *Wilsons & Clyde Coal Co Ltd v English* [1938] A.C. 57 at 78. There should be added: "a safe place of work" and it should also be borne in mind that a corporate employer still owes these obligations to an employee who is one of its directors or its sole director, see *Lee v Lee's Air Farming Ltd* [1961] A.C. 12; [1960] 3 W.L.R. 758 PC; and that it may also do so in appropriate cases where the employee is the majority shareholder, see *Clark v Clark Construction Initiatives Ltd* [2009] B.C.C. 665; [2008] I.C.R. 635 EAT. **12-03**

Nature of the duty: harm to health

Replace footnote 22 with:

[22] *Calveley v Chief Constable of Merseyside* [1989] A.C. 1228; [1989] 2 W.L.R. 624 HL, applied in *French v Sussex CC* [2004] EWHC 3217 (QB); [2005] P.I.Q.R. P18, for which see further, Ch.2, para.2-174. See also *T v W* [2022] CSOH 44: an employer did not know of a teacher's psychological vulnerability and could not have been expected to foresee that subjecting her to an assessment of classroom management skills and teaching competence coupled with the provision of appropriate mentoring and support would result in psychological injury. **12-06**

Duty is personal and not delegable

Replace footnote 37 with:

[37] See Ch.7, paras 7-106 to 7-108. See also *McDermid v Nash Dredging & Reclamation Co Ltd* [1987] A.C. 906 at 919; [1987] 3 W.L.R. 212 HL, per Lord Brandon: "The essential characteristic of the duty **12-10**

is that, if it is not performed, it is no defence for the employer to show that he delegated its performance to a person, whether his servant or not his servant, whom he reasonably believed to be competent to perform it. Despite such delegation the employer is liable for the non-performance of the duty." In *Carr v Brands Transport Ltd* [2022] EWHC 3167 (KB), a haulage company was liable to its employee (who was also sole director and an 80% shareholder) for the negligent failure of an independent contractor which it had engaged to carry out safety inspections to detect a defect in a guard rail which failed and caused him to fall from the upper deck of a car transporter. Liability was based both on the general principle of the employer being unable to delegate its responsibility for providing a safe place and safe system of work, and also under Lord Sumption's second category of cases discussed in *Woodland v Essex CC* [2013] UKSC 66; [2014] P.I.Q.R. P6. See further Ch.7, paras 7-111 and 7-112.

Statutory duty to insure

Replace footnote 50 with:

12-13 [50] Although the 1930 Act continues to apply where the defendant employer became insolvent and incurred liability to the claimant employee before 1 August 2016. See *Redman v Zurich Insurance Plc* [2017] EWHC 1919 (QB); [2018] P.I.Q.R. P2, followed in *Keegan v Independent Insurance Co Ltd* [2022] EWHC 1992 (QB). In *Brooks v Zurich Insurance Plc* [2022] EWHC 1170 (QB), the court considered that the question of whether the claimant had suffered actionable damage before 1 August 2016 was, in the context of a claim for damages for mesothelioma, one of mixed fact and law in an uncertain and developing area and as such unsuitable for summary determination.

(B) Elements of the duty

(i) Safe place of work

Common law duty compared with statutory duty

Replace footnote 146 with:

12-34 [146] See *Baker v Quantum Clothing Group Ltd* [2011] 1 W.L.R. 1003 SC, para.12-21 and Ch.13, para.13-176. *Baker* was applied in *Williams v University of Birmingham* [2012] P.I.Q.R. P4 CA (Civ Div), Ch.5, para.5-32 (mesothelioma allegedly contracted as a result of exposure to asbestos in 1974 from the lagging around central heating pipes). *Williams* was considered in *Bussey v 00654701 Ltd (formerly Anglia Heating Ltd)* [2018] EWCA Civ 243; [2018] P.I.Q.R. P11, para.12-81, where it was stressed that the finding in the former as to the levels of asbestos dust "acceptable" in 1974 should not be elevated into a rule of law. In *White v Secretary of State for Health and Social Care* [2022] EWHC 3082 (KB), the court considered that the approach in *Jeromson v Shell Tankers Ltd* [2001] EWCA Civ 101 required it to ask whether the risk of asbestos-related injury ought reasonably to have been foreseen by a reasonably prudent employer to the extent that it ought to have taken precautions or sought advice. After *Bussey*, this was a two-stage test. Firstly should the risk have been recognised and secondly should precautions have been taken or advice sought; the two stages were related so that there would be no liability in a case where advice, if sought, would have been that the risk of injury was sufficiently low as not to be worth troubling about. On the facts, low-dose exposure from bunsen burner mats in the period 1949 to 1960 did not give rise to a breach of the employer's duty. See also *Abraham v G Ireson & Son (Properties) Ltd* [2009] EWHC 1958 (QB) (low dose exposure from intermittent use of a plumber's scorch mat insufficient to establish breach of duty where advice would have concluded that the risk of injury was negligible) which was followed in *White*. See also *Cuthbert v Taylor Woodrow Construction Holdings* [2022] EWHC 3036 (KB), where the employer could not reasonably have foreseen a risk from light and intermittent exposure to asbestos in the 1950s.

(iii) Adequate plant and appliances

Inspections and maintenance

Replace footnote 217 with:

12-59 [217] For the importance of carrying out examinations, see *Pearce v Round Oak Steel Works* [1969] 1 W.L.R. 595 CA (Civ Div). If the apparatus is complicated, it may not be justifiable merely to rely upon the operator's inspecting it and reporting any faults that they can find: *Shotter v R&H Green & Silley Weir Ltd* [1951] 1 Lloyd's Rep. 329 KBD. See also *Storey v British Telecommunications Plc* [2022] EWCA Civ 616; [2022] P.I.Q.R. P15, where the Court of Appeal considered it arguable that an employer's failure to react adequately to a reported fault in acoustic equipment could found an action at common law for acoustic shock.

Chapter 13

LIABILITY FOR BREACH OF STATUTORY DUTY

Table of Contents

2. Categories of Breach of Statutory Duty

Illustrations

Replace paragraph 13-15 with:

The approach to liability in the second group, that is, where the focus is on how a statutory duty has been exercised in practice, was considered and modified by the Supreme Court in *Poole BC v GN*.[40] On reviewing the authorities that followed X (Minors) it was concluded that Caparo did not provide a universal test for the existence of a duty, but that an incremental approach was necessary, using the existing **13-15** law by analogy, and with the Caparo criteria assisting in the decision as to whether a duty was established on the facts. Public policy considerations alone are not determinative, and public authorities are subject to the same general principles of the law of negligence as private individuals, except to the extent that legislation requires a departure. Thus the mere existence of a statutory power or duty is not sufficient on its own to generate a common law duty unless the public authority has created the source of danger or assumed a responsibility to protect the claimant from harm.[41] *Poole* was followed in two subsequent cases where local authorities were alleged to owe duties to protect vulnerable children from harm. In *DFX v Coventry City Council*[42] the court stressed that at common law there is generally no liability for negligence in failing to protect from harm caused by third parties. In the result a claim was struck out where the pleadings disclosed no basis for leading evidence of any particular behavior by the defendant council from which an assumption of responsibility could be inferred other than the mere performance of its statutory functions. The same approach was taken in the cases of *HXA v Surrey CC* and *YXA v Wolverhampton City Council*[43] where claims framed as negligent acts were properly to be categorised as complaints of omission or failing to confer a benefit and as such were struck out because the claimants could not establish that the defendant local authority had assumed a responsibility to protect from harm.[44] The courts may be less prepared to recognise the possibility of a private law duty based on the assumption of responsibility in cases involving the acts or omissions of police officers. In *Tindall v Chief Constable of Thames Valley*,[44a] the Court of Appeal gave general guidance in the context of a claim arising out of consecutive road traffic accidents due to black ice. The police attended after the first accident and then left the road as they found it and did not take steps to prevent a further accident. The Court of Appeal reiterated that the duty of the police was to avoid causing damage and not to prevent future damage and would not be liable even where it had intervened ineffectually provided that they had not made matters worse. Knowledge of the danger was not sufficient to found liability and neither was the fact that the police had intervened in similar cases. It was useful to ask whether the relationship between the police and the claimant was any different to the relationship between the police and the generality of the relevant class of the general public. *Tindall* was followed in *CJ v Chief Constable of Wiltshire*,[44b] where the court declined to recognise a duty on the part of police officers to prevent the sexual abuse of five children by the same offender on the grounds that the case was one where the relevant acts and omissions fell to be categorised as allegations of failure to conder a benefit.

[40] *Poole BC v GN* [2019] UKSC 25; [2019] 2 W.L.R. 1478 (two children alleged negligence in the exercise of a local authority's investigative duties under the Children Act 1989: they had been housed next door to a family known for anti-social behavior which had resulted in verbal and physical abuse over the course of several years). See further Ch.2, paras 2-23, 2-371 and 2-372.

[41] On the facts of *Poole BC v GN*, the council's investigation and monitoring of the claimants' harassment and bullying at the hands of third parties did not amount to the provision of a service to them, on which they could be expected to rely. The claimants had not entrusted their safety to the council and so it could not be argued that the latter had assumed a responsibility to perform its statutory functions with reasonable care. In *Magill v Chief Constable of PSNI* [2022] NICA 49, a strike out application was narrowly avoided as a result of amendments alleging that the defendant created a danger to the claimant by virtue of the positive acts of its officers.

[42] *DFX v Coventry City Council* [2021] EWHC 1382 (QB); [2021] P.I.Q.R. P18.

[43] *YXA v Wolverhampton City Council* [2021] EWHC 2974 (QB). The decisions in both HXA and YXA were successfully appealed, the former on the grounds that the defendant's "keeping safe" duty could

arguably amount to "something more" and so found a duty based on the assumption of responsibility test in *Poole* and the latter on the grounds that an assumption of responsibility might arise when a child was voluntarily accommodated in respite care. The court declined to give general guidance and observed that such cases were always fact specific and that the applicable principles would be refined as the law developed: *HXA v Surrey CC* [2022] EWCA Civ 1196; [2023] P.I.Q.R. P4. The courts may be less prepared to recognise the possibility of a private law duty in cases involving the acts or omissions of police officers. In *Tindall v Chief Constable of Thames Valley* [2022] EWCA Civ 25; [2022] R.T.R. 16, the Court of Appeal did give general guidance in the context of a claim arising out of consecutive road traffic accidents due to black ice. The police attended after the first accident and then left the road as they found it and did not take steps to prevent a further accident. In *CJ v Chief Constable of Wiltshire* [2022] EWHC 1661 (QB); [2023] P.I.Q.R. P2, the court declined to recognise a duty on the part of police officers to prevent the sexual abuse of five children by the same offender on the grounds that the case was one where the relevant acts and omissions fell to be categorised as allegations of failure to conder a benefit. The court applied *Tindall.*

[44] See also *J v South Wales Local Authority* [2021] EWCA Civ 1102 where the Court of Appeal reversed a decision allowing a local authority to resile from longstanding admissions of the existence and breach of a common law duty to place the claimant for adoption as a baby: Poole did not establish that no such duty could ever exist, and the claimant had not pleaded facts relevant to an assumption of responsibility precisely because the nature of the admissions made this unnecessary.

[44a] *Tindall v Chief Constable of Thames Valley* [2022] EWCA Civ 25.

[44b] *CJ v Chief Constable of Wiltshire* [2022] EWHC 1661 (QB).

Replace footnote 59 with:

[59] *Seddon v Driver and Vehicle Licensing Agency* [2019] EWCA Civ 14; [2019] W.L.R. 4593. However, a local authority assumed a duty when it wrongly informed the claimant taxi driver in the course of discretionary pre-application advice that the car he proposed to purchase would meet its licensing criteria: see *Wokingham BC v Arshad* [2022] EWHC 2419 (KB); [2023] R.T.R. 9. The claim failed on the grounds that the local authority could not have foreseen that the claimant would suffer psychiatric illness as a result of the loss of revenue consequent on his failure to secure a licence. **13-19**

3. When an Action may be Brought

Another remedy provided for the breach

Replace footnote 190 with:

[190] *X (Minors) v Bedfordshire CC* [1995] 2 A.C. 633. See also *Houston v Transport for London* [2022] EWHC 3279 (KB), where the existence of a right of appeal was fatal to a private law claim under the Private Hire Vehicles (London) Act 1998. **13-50**

4. Civil Liability and Health and Safety Regulations

The impact of section 69

Replace paragraph 13-75 with:

It remains to be seen whether the standards as currently set by the various health and safety regulations and the approved Codes of Practice published by the Health and Safety Executive will be applied and adopted as the appropriate standard for the common law.[256] In *Cockerill v CXK Ltd*[257] the parties agreed that when considering the nature of an employer's common law duty it was still permissible to have regard to the statutory duties to understand what steps an employer could be expected to take. The trial judge did not disapprove of this approach but considered that care was required and although the statutory duties continue to be relevant to the question of what an employer ought reasonably to do, by enacting s.69 "Parliament evidently intended to make a perceptible change in the legal relationship between employers and employees".[258] In *Kennedy v Cordia (Services) LLP*[259] **13-75**

Lords Reed and Hodge considered that "the expansion of the statutory duties imposed on employers in the field of health and safety has given rise to a body of knowledge and experience in this field" which they thought created "the context in which the court has to assess an employer's performance of its common law duty of care".[260] Such an approach is consistent with those decisions where the existence of a statutory duty has been regarded as evidence of the state of knowledge of a reasonable (i.e. non negligent) employer as regards a particular risk.[261] It is also consistent with the decision of the Supreme Court in *Baker v Quantum Clothing Group Ltd*,[262] where the majority concluded that the criteria for liability under s.29 of the Factories Act were not significantly different from those for negligence at common law, having regard to the proviso for reasonable practicability and the burden of proof. Lord Dyson observed:[263]

> "I assume that the justification for saying that the statutory duty must differ from the common law duty is that the statutory provisions would otherwise be otiose. But there is no principle of law that a statutory obligation cannot be interpreted as being co-terminous with a common law duty. As Stephenson LJ said in *Bux v Slough Metals Ltd* [1973] 1 W.L.R. 1358, 1369-1370: 'The statutory obligation may exceed the duty at common law or it may fall short of it or it may equal it'. Sometimes Parliament may decide that, in the interests of clarity and certainty, there is advantage in providing a detailed all-embracing set of rules. The merit in setting these out in a single authoritative document, such as a statute, is not undermined even if they do no more than reflect what the courts would be likely to decide when applying the common law."

[256] Practitioners continue to plead breaches of statutory duty as "evidence of negligence". Before s.69 was implemented, during a Parliamentary debate on the Bill, Lord Faulks, Minister of State for Justice (as he then was), said: "A breach of a regulation will be regarded as strong prima facie evidence of negligence. Judges will need some persuasion that the departure from a specific and well-targeted regulation does not give rise to a claim in negligence". See *Cunningham v Rochdale MBC* [2021] EWCA Civ 1719, para.13-74.

[257] *Cockerill v CXK Ltd* [2018] EWHC 1155 (QB), Rice J. See P. Curran, "Pleading reliance on breaches of statutory duty post-ERRA" [2019] (1) J.P.I.L. 66–73. Contrast the rather more controversial case of *Tonkins v Tapp* unreported 7 December 2018 QBD, a decision of HH Judge Allan Gore QC sitting as a judge of the High Court. He considered the judgment in *Cockerill* and at [106] said: "Accordingly, I would not have been prepared to find, without much more analysis and argument, that the effect of section 69 [of the 2013 Act] was to deprive an accident victim of entitlement to rely upon a finding that breach of statutory duty constituted ipso facto negligence as constituting breach of the scope and standard of care reasonably required of the alleged tortfeasor by the statutory duty even if no civil right of action was available for its breach."

[258] *Cockerill v CXK Ltd* [2018] EWHC 1155 (QB) at [18], per Rice J.

[259] *Kennedy v Cordia (Services) LLP* [2016] UKSC 6; 2016 S.L.T. 209.

[260] *Kennedy v Cordia (Services) LLP*, 2016 S.L.T. 209 at [64]. See also *Carr v Brands Transport Ltd* [2022] EWHC 3167 (KB), where the court accepted that duties imposed by the Lifting Operations and Lifting Equipment Regulations 1998 (SI 1998/2307), the Provision and Use of Work Equipment Regulations 1998 (SI 1998/2306) and the Work at Height Regulations 2005 (SI 2005/735) assisted in defining the scope of the steps that a reasonable and prudent employer could have been expected to take in order to provide a reasonably safe workplace and system of work. The court took essentially the same position in *Chadwick v RH Ovenden Ltd* [2022] EWHC 1701 (QB).

[261] See per Smith LJ in *Allison v London Underground Ltd* [2008] EWCA Civ 71; [2008] P.I.Q.R. P10, discussed further at para.13-125. See also *Franklin v Gramophone Co Ltd* [1948] 1 K.B. 542 CA at 558, per Somervell LJ; *National Coal Board v England* [1954] A.C. 403 HL; and more recently *Griffiths v Vauxhall Motors Ltd* [2003] EWCA Civ 412. It can be argued that the duty to risk assess is in any event firmly established in the common law: *Uren v Corporate Leisure (UK) Ltd & MOD* [2011] EWCA Civ 66.

[262] *Baker v Quantum Clothing Group Ltd* [2011] UKSC 17; [2011] 1 W.L.R. 1003, para.13-174.

[263] *Baker v Quantum Clothing Group Ltd* [2011] 1 W.L.R. 1003 at [125].

Replace paragraph 13-76 with:

Nevertheless, there is still a notable lack of authority on the impact of s.69.[264] One factor which points to the continued importance of the health and safety regulations is that many of them carry criminal sanctions in the event of breach. It would seem difficult for an employer to argue that it had acted reasonably whilst at the same time being guilty of a crime for having fallen below the standards set by Parliament for the protection of the health and safety of employees. It is certainly difficult, if not impossible, to see how an employer could argue that harm was not foreseeable in the face of a statutory duty to take precautions against it eventuating. The burden on the employee would be to show that any injury sustained fell within the scope of the particular regulation. It appears that whilst courts are prepared in many cases to treat breaches of statutory duty as relevant to the standards to be expected of the reasonable and prudent employer towards his employee, the position may be somewhat different outside of the employment relationship. In *Lewin v Gray*,[264a] the court refused to treat a client's failure to ensure that his contractor produced a construction phase plan as required by reg.4(5) of the Construction (Design and Management) Regulations 2015 (SI 2015/51) as sufficient to establish negligence at common law, despite the fact that the breach could have been prosecuted as a criminal offence.[264b] **13-76**

[264] In the Scottish case of *Gichrist v Asda Stores Ltd* [2015] CSOH 77; 2015 Rep. L.R. 95, counsel for the pursuer argued that as employers remain under a statutory duty to comply with health and safety regulations, then those duties should define the scope of the duty at common law: that statutory duties remain relevant as evidence of standards expected of employers in civil cases and that an employer who breached a regulation and was committing an offence could not be acting reasonably. Counsel for the defender submitted that the 2013 Act must have some content but, according to the judge, "did not expand on his argument" and for this reason the judge accepted the pursuer's arguments. The decision does not set any precedent and the arguments about the law were ultimately immaterial to the decision. In *Wright v National Galleries of Scotland* [2020] SAC (Civ 6); 2020 S.L.T. (Sh Ct) 175, reg.17 of the Workplace Health, Safety and Welfare Regulations 1992 (SI 1992/3004) was said to inform the respondent's common law duty of care to those working at its premises. Gilchrist and Wright were followed in *McDonald v Indigo Sun Retail Ltd*, 2021 S.C.L.R 269; 2021 Rep. L.R. 60, where the court considered that the obligations imposed by the Control of Noise at Work Regulations 2005 (SI 2005/1643) were relevant to deciding the issue of breach of a duty of care at common law. The defendant's appeal was rejected on the grounds that the court below was entitled to conclude that breach of the Control of Noise at Work Regulations 2005 was sufficient to establish breach of duty at common law: *McDonald v Indigo Sun Retail Ltd* [2022] SAC (Civ) 15.

[264a] *Lewin v Gray* [2023] EWHC 112 (KB) (a self-employed roofing contractor was engaged to provide guttering to the roof of the defendant's barn. Whilst working at height, he fell through the roof and landed on the floor of the barn, sustaining catastrophic injuries. It was beyond doubt that neither the claimant nor the defendant had complied with the relevant health and safety regulations. The central issue was whether the defendant's failure could give rise to a cause of action in negligence). See also *Cockerill v CXK Ltd* [2018] EWHC 1155 (QB) and para.13-75.

[264b] Such a conviction could only be used to prove that such an offence had been committed, pursuant to s.11(1) of the Civil Evidence Act 1968. As it was admitted that the defendant had failed to ensure that a Construction Phase Plan had been completed, any criminal conviction would have been evidentially superfluous and, in any event, the defendant had not in fact been prosecuted or convicted. See also *Moreira v Moran* [2021] EWHC 1800 (QB); [2021] P.I.Q.R. P21. Breaches of health and safety regulations may be relevant as evidence of negligence but will not constitute negligence in and of themselves: see *Jagger v Holland* [2020] EWHC 46 (QB) and *Harris v Bartrums Haulage and Storage Ltd* [2020] EWHC 900 (QB).

5. BURDEN AND STANDARD OF PROOF OF A BREACH OF STATUTORY DUTY

Standard of proof

Replace footnote 300 with:

13-87 [300] *Hall v Edinburgh City Council*, 1999 S.L.T. 744 OH, in relation to the Manual Handling Operations Regulations 1992 (SI 1992/2793). See para.13-270. See also *Willock v Corus UK Ltd* [2013] EWCA Civ 519. Conversely an employer which is not in breach of statutory duty can still be liable to its employee at common law: see *Storey v British Telecommunications Plc* [2022] EWCA Civ 616; [2022] P.I.Q.R. P15, where the Court of Appeal was invited to strike out a claim for acoustic shock on the grounds that the claimant could not prove breach of the Control of Noise at Work Regulations 2005 but declined to do so on the grounds that it was arguable that the claimant's injury had been caused by pitch and acoustic pressure rather than sound level itself.

6. DEFENCES TO ACTION FOR BREACH OF STATUTORY DUTY

Momentary inattention or conscious acceptance of risk

Replace footnote 317 with:

13-92 [317] Per Pearce LJ in *Jenner v Allen West & Co Ltd* [1959] 1 W.L.R. 554 CA at 561. See M.H. Whincup, "Employees' Contributory Negligence" (1968) 118 New L.J. 972. See also *Mullard v Ben Line Steamers Ltd* [1970] 1 W.L.R. 1414 and Ch.4, para.4-72. For a recent case where a claimant employee's fault in failing to arrange for a safety inspection of a transporter lorry was held not to be co-extensive with his employer's failure to ensure a safe place and safe system of work (the employer being liable to the claimant by virtue of its having delegated these obligations to an incompetent independent contractor), despite the fact that the claimant was the sole director of the employer company, owned 80% of the shareholding and had himself engaged the independent contractor, see *Carr v Brands Transport Ltd* [2022] EWHC 3167 (KB). The court held that the claimant had "a lot on his plate" in setting up the fledgling company and found that "to err is human". The claimant was however guilty of contributory negligence of 40% of the value of his claim.

Chapter 14

DANGEROUS THINGS: RYLANDS V FLETCHER

Table of Contents

3. Water

Liability for accumulating water

Replace paragraph 14-59 with:

On the other hand, if a person who is a natural user of land accumulates water on it, for example in a pond or a stream, there is no liability under *Rylands v Fletcher* for damage caused by its overflow.[226] The same applies where a landowner does something on his own land, such as digging a trench to lay a pipe,[227] which causes water naturally on the land to flow more quickly onto his neighbour's land, provided that he does not collect it in any way. But if he causes more water to be discharged from his land onto his neighbour's land than would normally be the case, or collects the drainage of his land into one place and discharges it onto his neighbour's land, he will be liable.[228] Thus, developers who had altered a rear garden by adding spoil to the lawn area to level it, and building a rockery slope and a paved area, were liable for causing persistent, severe flooding to the neighbours' rear garden.[228a] The essence of the claimants' case was that the flooding to their rear garden was caused by the increase in water flow from the adjacent property due to **14-59** the developers' construction works.[228b] As already noted,[229] a landowner is entitled to abstract subterranean water flowing in undefined channels beneath his land, regardless of the consequences to his neighbours.[230]

[226] The decision that there had been a natural user of land in *Rouse v Gravelworks Ltd* [1940] 1 K.B. 489 CA where water had accumulated in a quarry was criticised in *Leakey v National Trust* [1980] Q.B. 485 CA (Civ Div), the CA preferring *Davey v Harrow Corp* [1958] 1 Q.B. 60 CA where the encroachment of roots and branches onto a neighbour's land causing damage gave the neighbour an action in nuisance.

[227] *Barlett v Tottenham* [1932] 1 Ch. 114 Ch D: an underground spring was tapped with the result that water was discharged on to the claimant's land.

[228] *Hurdman v North Eastern Railway Co* (1878) 3 C.P.D. 168 CA, *Whalley v L&Y Railway Co* (1884) 13 Q.B.D. 131 CA.

[228a] *Partakis-Stevens v Sihan* [2022] EWHC 3249 (TCC) (the current owners who had purchased the property from the developers were also liable given that the provision of a slot drain would have been a reasonable solution to the problem. An injunction was granted requiring them to undertake those drainage works).

[228b] This engaged the principle derived from *Hurdman v North Eastern Railway Co* (1878) 3 C.P.D. 168, which was cited by Viscount Maugham in *Sedleigh Denfield v O'Callaghan* [1940] A.C. 880 HL as one of three cases in support of the proposition that there is a distinction between a natural use of land or of water flowing through it and the consequences of constructing some artificial work on land which alters the flow of water and causes damage to a neighbour.

[229] See Ch.2 para.2-140.

[230] *Chetwynd v Tunmore* [2016] EWHC 156 (QB); [2016] Env. L.R. 23 (no liability in negligence or nuisance where it was alleged that accumulating water in four lakes caused a significant decrease in the levels of lakes on adjoining land which were used as a commercial fishery; a claim under the Water Resources Act 1991 s.48A also failed, "but for" causation not being made out).

Sewers and drains

After paragraph 14-91, add new paragraph:

14-91a The owner of development land next to a railway station recovered damages for nuisance caused by a collapsed drain under the railway land and consequent flooding, which had prevented it from proceeding with the development as planned. The station owner knew that the drainage system needed an overhaul, and even applying a "measured duty of care", as developed in cases of natural nuisance, it should have prioritised the remediation works when put on notice of the flooding.[320a] Considerations of fairness, justice and reasonableness as between neighbouring landowners led to the conclusion that there was liability even if the duty owed was "measured".

[320a] *House Maker (Padgate) Ltd v Network Rail Infrastructure* [2022] EWHC 1482 (TCC) (although the court was hesitant about applying a "measured duty of care" in cases where an artificial culvert or drain had collapsed, the concepts of reasonableness and foreseeability of harm were the same and therefore made no practical difference to the outcome); see also *Delaware Mansions Ltd v Westminster City Council* [2001] UKHL 55; [2002] 1 A.C. 321.

CHAPTER 15

ANIMALS

TABLE OF CONTENTS

2. STRICT LIABILITY FOR DAMAGE DONE BY ANIMALS GENERALLY

Non-dangerous species

Replace list in paragraph 15-13 with:

(a) *The damage is of a kind which the animal, unless restrained, was likely to cause or which, if caused by the animal, was likely to be severe.*[44] **15-13**

Section 2(2)(a) of the 1971 Act is relatively straightforward. There are two limbs to the test. In order to succeed, a claimant has to satisfy at least one of them.[44a] The first limb is illustrated by the facts of *Kite v Napp*[45] where an Irish Wolfhound, named Prince, had a propensity to go after people with bags. The claimant was walking home, carrying a hold-all, when she was approached by Prince, who was roaming free in the street, and bitten on the leg. It was held that, given his propensity, Prince was likely to cause such damage unless restrained. In *Curtis v Betts*[46] where a young bull mastiff dog bit a 10-year-old boy on the face, he was found to be an animal of a kind which would satisfy s.2(2)(a) since the damage, if caused by the dog, was likely to be severe.[47] *Hunt v Wallis*[48] is an example of the second limb. A border collie was not likely to cause physical injury but, since it ran into the claimant, given its size and speed, if it did cause damage *this was likely to be severe*, thus satisfying the second limb of s.2(2)(a). It should be noted that there is no requirement that the damage should in fact be severe: the test is one of foreseeability of damage.[49] **15-14**

"Likely" means "reasonably to be expected" not "more probable that not".[50] The question of whether or not severe injury is reasonably to be expected is a factual matter for determination on the evidence presented at trial. Neither the likelihood of injury, nor the severity of it, should be assumed from the circumstances of the accident or the fact that the claimant did, in fact, suffer a severe injury.[50a] These are issues that require prospective consideration and cannot be assumed with the benefit of hindsight.[50b] In making that determination, the court is entitled to rely upon expert evidence in relation to the animal's behaviour and characteristics.[50c]

15-15 It appears debatable whether a fall from a rearing horse will necessarily satisfy the second limb of s.2(2)(a). The point was conceded or readily assumed in a number of cases.[51] Recent authorities, however, suggest that in many cases this may not be assumed and evidence on the point a necessary precursor to making such a finding.[52] In *Bodey v Hall*,[53] the court held that the second limb of s.2(2)(a) of the 1971 Act was satisfied without receiving expert evidence on the subject. In that case, a groom travelling in a pony and trap was injured when the pony bolted and the trap tipped. The court held that the question as to whether an injury caused by the pony was likely to be severe ought to be answered by reference to the circumstances of the accident, thus concluding that a fall from trap pulled by a bolting horse was likely to cause severe injury. But this approach can give rise to a difficulty, succinctly expressed by Lewison LJ in another case:

> "The problem, as I see it, is the level of generality at which you ask and answer the question. If the question is: if you fall off a rearing horse onto a hard surface, and the horse falls on top of you, is the injury likely to be severe, you may get one answer. But if the question is: if you fall off a horse is the injury likely to be severe, you may get another. I do not believe that this problem has yet been squarely confronted in the cases."[54]

He went on:

> "Almost anyone who has ever ridden will have the experience of having fallen off a horse, getting up and remounting the horse. I do not, with respect, regard it as self-evident that a rider who falls off a rearing horse or, for that matter, a cantering horse, is likely to suffer severe injury."[55]

15-16 In *Lynch v ED Walker Racing Ltd*[56] the court considered that the level of particularity at which one asked the question as to the likelihood of severe damage was important, indicating that it could not be at a level where the circumstances of the accident answered the question but neither could it be completely divorced from the facts of the case. The court said:

> "Where precisely to place it must permit the sections of statute to have some meaning and effect as has been pointed out in the authorities. If section 2(2)(a) is to be capable of separate answer from 2(2)(b) the fact that, in the circumstances, an animal causes serious injury cannot show that any injury likely to be caused would be serious."[57]

15-17 In *Lynch* the claimant rider was injured falling from his horse after it whipped round, lost its footing, possibly because of the presence of a nearby bank, and fell onto its side. A decision that in these circumstances there was no liability, as severe injury was not reasonably to be expected and the damage was not of a kind which the animal, unless restrained, was likely to cause, was upheld on appeal. These issues were regarded as issues of fact, not law, and there was support for such an outcome in the expert evidence adduced at trial.[58]

(b) *The likelihood of the damage or of its being severe was due to characteristics of the animal which are not normally found in animals of the same species or are not normally so found except at particular times or in particular circumstances*.[59]

The requirements set out in s.2(2)(b) of the 1971 Act both depend upon abnormal characteristics. The first part of the subsection is concerned with an animal that has characteristics which are not normally found in animals of that species. This arises in cases where animals of this species are normally docile but the animal which caused the damage is not. Abnormal characteristics can, but do not necessarily, comprise a vicious tendency based on past conduct,[60] or simply unusual characteristics. Thus, in *Wallace v Newton*,[61] where the claimant, a groom in the defendant's training stables, was crushed and seriously injured, while attempting to lead a thoroughbred show-jumper into a horse-box trailer, it was held that in order to succeed, it was not necessary that the horse had any vicious tendency to attack people, but only that it had particular characteristics of unpredictability and unreliability unusual in a horse and in that way dangerous, and that it was from those characteristics that injury arose. Similarly, where the claimant had been bitten by a dog, which was known to attack people carrying bags, it was held to possess a characteristic peculiar to itself within the meaning of para.(b).[62] By way of contrast, in *Fitzgerald v Cooke (ED and AD) Bourne (Farms)*, a pre-Act case, the claimant's claim failed where the court was satisfied that in knocking the claimant to the ground, a young unbroken thoroughbred filly was indulging in a natural propensity to be playful, rather than viciousness.[63] **15-18**

The second, alternative, requirement of s.2(2)(b) of the 1971 Act has given rise to difficulty and led to two different lines of authority.[64] For liability to arise under this part of the section the abnormal dangerous characteristic of the animal must be one which is not a characteristic of animals of that species save on particular occasions. This gave rise to the question as to whether the keeper of an animal is strictly liable for damage caused by the animal when its behaviour in the circumstances was not abnormal for an animal of that species in those circumstances. More than 30 years after the passing of the Act, the House of Lords had an opportunity to resolve this question in *Mirvahedy v Henley*.[65] The case arose from a collision on a road between a car and a horse, one of several that had panicked for some unknown reason and escaped from a field, pushing over an electric fence and travelling over a mile before they reached the road. It was agreed that while this behaviour was not normal for horses in normal circumstances, it was usual when such animals were alarmed or under threat. Thus, by a majority, it was held that the second limb of the subsection did indeed apply to temporary characteristics which were nevertheless normal for the animal in particular circumstances, even if those circumstances were unusual. Lord Hobhouse said: **15-19**

> "It is true that there is an implicit assumption of fact in section 2(2) that domesticated animals are not normally dangerous. But the purpose of paragraph (b) is to make provision for those that are. It deals with two specific categories where that assumption of fact is falsified. The first is that of an animal which is possessed of a characteristic, not normally found in animals of the same species, which makes it dangerous. The second is an animal which, although belonging to a species which does not normally have dangerous characteristics, nevertheless had dangerous characteristics at particular times or in particular circumstances. The essence of those provisions is the falsification of the assumption, in the first because of the departure of the individual from the norm for its species, in the second because of the introduction of special factors."[66]

In reaching this decision, Lord Nicholls acknowledged public policy considerations:

> "Considered as a matter of social policy, there are arguments in favour of [imposing strict liability for damage caused by the animal when the animal's behaviour was not abnormal for an animal of the species in those circumstances]. It may be said that the loss should fall on the person who chooses to keep an animal which is known to be dangerous in some circumstances. He is aware of the risks involved, and he should bear the risk. On the other hand, it can be said, that negligence apart, everyone must take the risks associated with the ordinary characteristics of animals commonly kept in this country."[67]

15-20 Before a claim on the basis of strict liability under the 1971 Act can attach, it has to be shown that the characteristic of the animal which is causative of damage to the claimant is a dangerous behavioural characteristic, even though only exhibited at particular times or in particular circumstances.[67a] Where a cow escaped from a field on to a road and, whilst stationary on the road was struck by a car, a claim for the death of the passenger and injury to the driver failed. The behavioural characteristic relied on by the claimants, agitation resulting from the cow's normal maternal instinct upon being separated from her calf, was itself neither dangerous nor causative. The cow's dangerous and causative behaviour, which included climbing a six bar livestock gate and crossing a 12 foot cattle grid, reflected exceptional and exaggerated agitation, so that she was in the state of an excited wild animal, was held to be not a characteristic for the cow or its breed and not a characteristic known to the defendant.[68] Similarly, there was no liability where a taxi struck a loose horse on the A3 causing catastrophic injuries to an innocent passenger.[68a] Immediately prior to the collision the horse was found to have been either stationary or barely moving and there was no evidence that she was frightened to the point of panic or that she was fleeing from a perceived threat. Whereas the horse may have been somewhat agitated earlier in the day, it is likely that she had recovered quickly from that agitation and was not panicked[68b] when the collision occurred. As such, the court could not find that the likelihood of the damage to the claimant, or of its being severe, was due to characteristics not normally found in horses except at particular times or in particular circumstances. Rather, it was due to the horse being a large and heavy animal who was standing on a dual carriageway where she should not have been. By way of contrast, where a Charolais steer became startled, escaped from a farm and got onto a road some one and half miles away where it was in collision with a car, the driver of the car succeeded in his claim for personal injuries. In the light of expert evidence that the steer would have remained frightened and unpredictable throughout its journey and the finding that it was probably running in panic on the carriageway at the time of the collision, it was held that the damage was attributable to the steer behaving in a dangerous way in the particular circumstances of having been spooked by various adverse stimuli, which can happen in such circumstances. It did not matter whether the steer ran into the driver or vice versa: the accident was caused by this dangerous characteristic.[69]

15-21 The importance of identifying the relevant causative characteristic is illustrated in the cases. Where a normally obedient horse stepped into the road contrary to the direction of the rider and collided with the claimant's car, resulting in damage to the car and personal injury to the driver, it was held that whilst the damage was of a kind which, if caused, was likely to be severe due to the size of the horse, the likelihood of the damage or its being severe was due to a normal characteristic of the animal, i.e. its weight, and not to a characteristic not normally found in horses except at particular times and in particular circumstances. Indeed, it was doubted, on appeal, whether a propensity to move occasionally otherwise than as directed could be described as a characteristic.[70] In contrast, where an otherwise well behaved horse reared up when its rider, who was reasonably proficient but lacked experience, tried to get the horse to go forward at a cross roads, causing the claimant rider to fall and there was evidence that it is normal equine behaviour for a horse to rear in such circumstances, the rider's claim succeeded as the relevant characteristic was held to be the propensity to rear when the animal did not want to go forward and was being ridden by someone who was unable to handle him and give him confidence. It was held that the core meaning of "normally" in "characteristics ... which are not normally found ...." was "conforming to type". Thus if a characteristic was usual then it would certainly be normal. The Court of Appeal said that it was difficult to see why Parliament should have intended to exclude from the ambit of s.2(2)(b) cases where the relevant characteristic was natural, although unusual, in the animal which caused the damage. If s.2(2)(b) was interpreted in that way, there was nothing unjust or unreasonable, as between the keeper, who could decide whether to run the unavoidable risks involved in keeping horses, and whether or not to insure against those risks, and the victim of the horse's behaviour, in requiring the keeper to bear the loss.[71]

That reasoning was applied where a claimant fell from a horse which had a habit of bucking when going into a canter.[72] The relevant characteristic for the purposes of s.2(2)(b) was said to be bucking, not bucking when going into a canter, as considerations of time and circumstances were only relevant elements in the second, alternative, limb of s.2(2)(b) and, thus the core meaning of "normal" was "conforming to type" and the judge had been entitled to find on the evidence that the claimant had failed to establish that bucking was not a normal characteristic of horses generally. Under the second limb of s.2(2)(b), the relevant question was whether it was normal for horses generally to buck at particular times and in particular circumstances, including when beginning to canter. The words "at particular times or in particular circumstances" denoted times or circumstances that could be described and predicted. Since there was no evidence that horses generally bucked at particular times or in particular circumstances, the claim failed. **15-22**

The Court of Appeal further examined the interpretation and application of the second limb of s.2(2)(b)[73] in *Ford v Seymour-Williams*,[74] and again in the context of a horse causing injury by rearing. The claimant was attending a pre-season autumn meet of the Duke of Beaufort's Hounds at Badminton and riding the defendant's horse, a 19-year-old gelding called Tommy. Some 20 or 30 m after trotting into a field, the horse suddenly stopped, stepping back or sideways but refusing to go forwards. The claimant encouraged him to proceed but the horse reared up, fell over backwards and landed on top of her. The horse struggled on the ground for some five or six minutes before dying. The experts at trial were unable to ascertain exactly why the horse reared, but they postulated two possibilities: disobedience or a cardiovascular catastrophe. It **15-23** was common ground that the requirements of s.2(2)(a) were satisfied and the first limb of s.2(2)(b) were not. The question was whether or not the requirements of the second limb of s.2(2)(b) and then s.2(2)(c) were met. The claimant submitted that identifying the particular circumstance of the rearing was irrelevant for the purposes of s.2(2)(b) on the basis that, whichever circumstance applied, the rearing was within the boundaries of normal equine behaviour. In rejecting her appeal, the Court of Appeal considered that the authorities[75] demonstrate that it is necessary to identify not only the characteristic but also the particular time or circumstance in which it arose. Fundamentally, s.2(2)(b) needs to be construed in the context of s.2 as a whole and the identification of the particular time or circumstance in question is necessary for an assessment of whether or not a keeper has the relevant knowledge for the purpose of s.2(2)(c). Adopting this approach, on the facts, the conditions in s.2(2)(b) were me—the evidence established that the likelihood of the damage was due to characteristics (namely rearing) not normally found in horses except at particular times or in particular circumstances—including a catastrophic internal injury, which the trial judge found as having been the probable cause and therefore the likely circumstance resulting in the rearing. By the same logic however, the knowledge required by s.2(2)(c) had to extend to the particular time when, or circumstance in which, the characteristic arose. The experts agreed that they had not known catastrophic internal injury to be the cause of rearing, but that it was theoretically possible. In light of the defendant's evidence that he had no professional experience of a horse rearing when in pain, the judge was entitled to find that the existence of what was only a theoretical possibility did not establish the knowledge necessary for the purposes of s.2(2)(c) and the claim failed on that basis.

15-24 It follows that, on establishing a pattern of behaviour capable of amounting to a dangerous "characteristic" in any given case, the characteristic so identified will either be abnormal, or normal at particular times or in particular circumstances: either way it will fall within one of the limbs of s.2(2)(b) and satisfy the requirement, and provided that it is causative of the damage the defendants will be left to argue, if they can, over whether the requirements of s.2(2)(a) and (c) have been met.[76] Many earlier cases have now to be reconsidered in the light of *Mirvahedy*.[77] In relation to a relatively recent example, *Gloster v Chief Constable of Greater Manchester Police*,[78] the suggestion that a police dog, which bit in accordance with its training, was responding to that training, rather than an inculcated propensity to bite, was expressly disapproved.[79]

15-25 Where the evidence suggested that a horse could buck when startled or alarmed, that was a sufficient characteristic for purposes of s.2(2)(b) of the Animals Act 1971[80] likewise where a horse pulling a trap shot forward unexpectedly in response to an unknown stimulus and thereby tilted the trap, causing the claimant to fall out.[81] In *Turnbull v Warrener*[82] there was disagreement whether evidence indicating that horses could display exuberance when first introduced to a bitless bridle, satisfied s.2(2)(b) of the Act, given that such a response occurred in less than 1 per cent of horses. On one view:

> "A characteristic of an animal was something that was inherent in that animal. An unprecedented, one-off action of an animal was not something inherent in the

animal. It was difficult to say of something that occurred in less than 1% of horses fitted with bitless bridles, that it was characteristic of them at particular times or in particular circumstances."[83]

On another view:

"The judge accepted that 'the reason why [Ms Turnbull] was unable to stop him was that she was trying to do it by means of a piece of equipment, namely the bitless bridle, to which Gem was unaccustomed'. This ought to have led to consideration of whether refusing to respond to instructions given through the bitless bridle was a characteristic of horses unfamiliar with such equipment. In my judgment, such consideration would or should have resulted in the answer that it was such a characteristic. But a refusal to respond to instructions given through the bitless bridle could be a characteristic of horses unfamiliar with such equipment."[84]

(c) *Those characteristics were known to that keeper or were at any time known to a person who at that time had charge of the animal as that keeper's servant or, where that keeper is the head of a household, were known to another keeper of the animal who is a member of that household and under the age of 16.*[85]

The knowledge required to impose liability is the actual knowledge of the keeper or that to be imputed to him, through a particular employee or agent.[86] So, where only one of two keepers of a horse was aware that it had a propensity to be frightened of farm machinery and the keeper without such knowledge was killed when thrown from the horse, the keeper with knowledge was liable to the deceased's widower for her death. A submission that the two keepers' knowledge of the horse's characteristics be treated as being the same, was rejected.[87] It is not sufficient to prove that the keeper ought to have known of the propensity.[88] There is no definition of knowledge contained in the Act so that reference back to the common law must be made for assistance.[89] What is required is knowledge of characteristics of the animal that indicate a tendency to cause the damage or injury which in fact ensues.[90] Separate consideration is required of the knowledge: (i) of the keeper himself; (ii) of his servant in charge; and (iii) of another keeper, who is a member of his household. Outside the confines of these categories, knowledge *cannot* be attributed to the keeper, under the 1971 Act. **15-26**

[44] Section 2(2)(a) of the 1971 Act.

[44a] It should be remembered that the burden of proof rests on the claimant to prove either of the limbs of s.2(2)(a): see *Schoultz v Ball* [2022] EWHC 2452 (KB) at [15], per HH Judge Clarke.

[45] *Kite v Napp Times* 1 June 1982 QBD.

[46] *Curtis v Betts* [1990] 1 W.L.R. 459.

[47] But see John Marston and Barbara Freer, "Dogs in Tort" (1990) L.S. Gaz., 5 Sep, 87 (26) where it is argued that as it was established that the mastiff was likely to react fiercely when defending his territory and the defendant considered it necessary to restrain him and thus knew of his instincts, it should have followed that liability was made out on the basis that the damage was of a kind the dog was likely to cause unless restrained.

[48] *Hunt v Wallis* [1994] P.I.Q.R. P128 QBD: Pill J held that in the light of the definition of "species" in s.11 of the Act, where an identifiable breed of dog existed such as "Border Collie", the relevant comparison ought to be made with that breed of dog and not dogs generally. See Exall, "Give a Dog a Bad Name", 135 S.J. 644.

[49] A child, who suffered a fractured humerus when thrown from a riding school pony, failed to establish that the damage caused was of a kind which a pony was likely to cause, or if it caused, was likely to be severe: *E v Townfoot Stables* [2004] C.L.Y. 169 CC.

[50] *Mirvahedy v Henley* [2003] 2 A.C. 491 at [95]–[97] per Lord Scott. Although Lord Scott's remarks were strictly obiter, in *Turnbull v Warrener* [2012] P.I.Q.R. P16. Maurice Kay LJ at [12] said that it was now well settled that "likely" meant "reasonably to be expected." See also *Lynch v Ed Walker Racing Ltd* [2017] EWHC 2484 (QB) at [13]–[16] .

[50a] *Schoultz v Ball* [2022] EWHC 2452 (KB) at [16], per HH Judge Clarke and see also *Lynch v Ed Walker Racing Ltd* [2017] EWHC 2484 (QB) at [24], per Langstaff J.

[50b] *Schoultz v Ball* [2022] EWHC 2452 (KB) at [16], per HH Judge Clarke.

[50c] *Lynch v Ed Walker Racing Ltd* [2017] EWHC 2484 (QB) at [55] and [62], per Langstaff J. For a discussion on the benefits of instructing an expert with practical experience over a largely academic expert without such a grounding, see *Schoultz v Ball* [2022] EWHC 2452 (KB) at [49], per HH Judge Clarke.

[51] *Welsh v Stokes* [2007] EWCA Civ 796; [2007] P.I.Q.R. P27 at [33], per Dyson LJ; *Clark v Bowlt* [2006] EWCA Civ 1185 at [11], per Lord Philips CJ. In *Freeman v Higher Park Farm* [2008] EWCA Civ 1185; [2009] P.I.Q.R. P6 at [34], Etherton LJ thought it unnecessary and unrealistic to require evidence that a fall from a horse was likely cause severe injury, he thought it "obvious that if a horse bucks so that the rider falls off, it is reasonably to be expected a severe injury will result." See also *Ford v Seymour-Williams* [2021] EWCA Civ 1848; [2022] P.I.Q.R. P7 and see paras 15-23 and 15-30.

[52] *Turnbull v Warrener* [2012] P.I.Q.R. P16 at [11]–[16], [52]–[54].

[53] *Bodey v Hall* [2011] EWHC 2162 (QB); [2012] P.I.Q.R. P1 at [33].

[54] *Turnbull v Warrener* [2012] P.I.Q.R. P16 at [51]. See further *Kublin v Jane Allison Equestrian Ltd* LTL 6/12/2013.

[55] *Turnbull v Warrener* [2012] P.I.Q.R. P16 at [54].

[56] *Lynch v ED Walker Racing Ltd* [2017] EWHC 2484 (QB).

[57] *Lynch v ED Walker Racing Ltd* [2017] EWHC 2484 (QB) at [24], per Langstaff J.

[58] *Lynch v ED Walker Racing Ltd* [2017] EWHC 2484 (QB) at [32], [55] and [62], per Langstaff J.

[59] Section 2(2)(b) of the 1971 Act.

[60] e.g. *Parsons v King* (1891) 8 T.L.R. 114.

[61] *Wallace v Newton* [1982] 1 W.L.R. 375 QBD. The horse was called "Lord Justice".

[62] *Kite v Napp, Times,* 1 June 1982 QBD; see also *Flack v Hudson* [2001] EWCA Civ 360; [2001] Q.B. 698: a horse liable to bolt when in the vicinity of agricultural machinery.

[63] *Fitzgerald v Cooke (ED and AD) Bourne (Farms)* [1964] 1 Q.B. 249; [1963] 3 W.L.R. 522 CA. The decision was distinguished in *Morris v Bailey* (1970) 13 D.L.R. (3d) 150 CA, where the defendant allowed his collie dog to run at large, knowing it had a propensity to run up to people barking furiously, although it stopped short of actually knocking them to the ground. See further *Welsh v Brady* [2008] CSOH 45; 2008 S.L.T. 363.

[64] *Breeden v Lampart* unreported 21 March 1985 and *Cummings v Grainger* [1977] Q.B. 397. For a discussion of the two lines of authority see *Mirvahedy v Henley* [2003] 2 A.C. 491 at [24]–[27], per Lord Nicholls.

[65] *Mirvahedy v Henley* [2003] 2 A.C. 491. See K. Amirthalingam, "Animal Liability—equine, canine and asinine" (2003) 119 L.Q.R. 563; D. Howarth, "The House of Lords and the Animals Act: closing the stable door" (2003) 62 C.L.J. 548; Barker, "Animals: where should the loss lie?" (2006) 4(9) E.P.S. 9.

[66] *Mirvahedy v Henley* [2003] 2 A.C. 491 at [71].

[67] *Mirvahedy v Henley* [2003] 2 A.C. 491 at 503, [6]. See further *Civil Liability for Animals*, 2nd edn (Oxford: OUP, 2012), Ch.2.

[67a] See *Mirvahedy v Henley* [2003] 2 A.C. 491 at [40]; see also *Schoultz v Ball* [2022] EWHC 2452 (KB) at [19], per HH Judge Clarke.

[68] *McKenny v Foster (t/a Foster Partnership)* [2008] EWCA Civ 173.

[68a] *Schoultz v Ball* [2022] EWHC 2452 (KB).

[68b] Interestingly, HH Judge Clarke, at [31], considered that not just any level of fear experienced by the horse would satisfy the test in s.2 and that the claimant would have to show that the horse was frightened

to the point of panic, or terrified, or distressed by fear, or otherwise severely frightened and that this was causative of the unusual behaviour which in turn was causative of the damage. See also *Mirvahedy v Henley* [2003] 2 A.C. 491 at [69], per Lord Hobhouse and at [137], per Lord Walker.

69 *Williams v Hawkes* [2017] EWCA Civ 1846; [2018] R.T.R. 16. It was also suggested that liability would have been made out in this case even if the steer, having run in panic, had been static at the time of collision, see Davies LJ at [38].

70 *Clark v Bowlt* [2006] EWCA Civ 978; [2007] P.I.Q.R. P12.

71 *Welsh v Stokes* [2007] P.I.Q.R. P27.

72 *Freeman v Higher Park Farm* [2009] P.I.Q.R. P6.

73 And also s.2(2)(c) of the 1971 Act.

74 *Ford v Seymour-Williams* [2022] P.I.Q.R. P7.

75 The Court of Appeal considered in detail the facts of *Mirvahedy v Henley* [2003] 2 A.C. 491; *Welsh v Stokes* [2007] P.I.Q.R. P27; *Freeman v Higher Park Farm* [2009] P.I.Q.R. P6; *Goldsmith v Patchcott* [2012] EWCA Civ 183; [2012] P.I.Q.R. P11; and *Turnbull v Warrener* [2012] P.I.Q.R. P16.

76 The Animals Act 1971 (Amendment) Bill, which proposed amending s.2 to limit the scope of *Mirvahedy* by affording keepers of animals a defence if they could show that there was no particular reason to expect an animal to react as it did, failed to attract sufficient Parliamentary support in March 2008.

77 e.g. *Jaundrill v Gillett, Times,* 30 January 1996 CA (Civ Div) (keeper not liable where an intruder maliciously opened a roadside field gate and, during the hours of darkness, drove out a number of horses which panicked and galloped along the highway into collision with an oncoming car). Said to be a decision on its own facts and of no general application in *Williams v Hawkes* [2018] R.T.R. 16.

78 *Gloster v Chief Constable of Greater Manchester Police* [2000] P.I.Q.R. P114.

79 Thus Lord Scott said, at [126]: "If biting at its handler's command is a characteristic of German Shepherds only after they have been trained to do so, it is not a normal characteristic of the subspecies."

80 *Goldsmith v Patchcott* [2012] P.I.Q.R. P11.

81 *Bodey v Hall* [2012] P.I.Q.R. P1. See further para.15-51.

82 *Turnbull v Warrener* [2012] P.I.Q.R. P16, fn.83.

83 *Turnbull v Warrener* [2012] P.I.Q.R. P16 at [40], [54], per Stanley Burnton LJ. See further, Regan, "Horsing around" 162 N.L.J. 769; B. Compton and J. Hand, "The Animals Act 1971—the statutory defences to strict liability" (2012) 1 J.P.I. Law 18.

84 *Turnbull v Warrener* [2012] P.I.Q.R. P16 at [21], per Maurice Kay LJ.

85 Section 2(2)(c) of the 1971 Act.

86 See s.2(2)(c) of the 1971 Act.

87 *Flack v Hudson* [2001] Q.B. 698.

88 *Mason v Keeling* (1699) 12 Mod. 332.

89 See *Glanville v Sutton* [1928] 1 K.B. 571 and *Brock v Richards* [1951] 1 K.B. 529 CA.

90 See *Smith v Ainger Times* 5 June 1990 CA (Civ Div) (the keeper of a dog with a known propensity to attack other dogs was liable to a claimant who was knocked over and hurt as it rushed to attack her own animal; it was incorrect to hold that knowledge of his animal's aggressive tendencies towards other dogs was insufficient to fix the defendant with knowledge of a characteristic which caused the claimant's injury). See further *McKenny v Foster (t/a Foster Partnership)* [2008] EWCA Civ 173, para.15-20 (a cow separated from her calf behaved in an exceptional way resulting from her maternal instinct, but the potential for such behaviour had not been known to the defendants: neither the cow, nor the breed generally, were known to exhibit such exaggerated anxiety as was shown, on the relevant occasion).

CHAPTER 16

PRODUCT LIABILITY

TABLE OF CONTENTS

2. LIABILITY IN CONTRACT

Strict Liability in Consumer Contracts

After "Act 2015 s.9.", add new footnote 35a:

[35a] For an example of a case concerning s.9, see *Kynaston-Mainwaring v GVE London Ltd* [2022] EWCA Civ 1339. **16-13**

3. LIABILITY UNDER THE CONSUMER PROTECTION ACT

(A) Under the Consumer Protection Act 1987: Part I "Product Liability"

Definition of "product"

After "the distribution system.", add new footnote 75a:

[75a] In *Pearson v Northern Powergrid (Northeast) Plc* unreported 26 April 2022 CC (Middlesbrough), HH Judge Mark Gargan refused to strike out a claim under the Consumer Protection Act 1987 where a power surge caused damage to electrical and electronic devices. He rejected the argument that electricity could only refer to force or current generated at the power station, and held it to be arguable that the defendant produced "domestic electricity" (a species of electricity under the Act) by "carrying out the process which has converted the electricity as generated into low voltage power which can be utilised in a domestic setting." **16-27**

An Objective Approach to Defect?

Replace paragraph 16-37 with:

16-37 There is clearly a conflict of approach between *A* and *Wilkes*. In cases subsequent to *Wilkes* the approach in *Wilkes* has been preferred.[109] In *Hastings v Finsbury Orthopaedics Ltd*, the Supreme Court approved the approach in *Wilkes*, stating:

> "The test of whether a product is defective is whether the safety of the product is not such as persons generally are entitled to expect. The test is not what is expected but one of entitled expectation. The test is an objective one. The standard of safety is measured by what the public at large is entitled to expect."[109a]

[109] In *Gee v DePuy International Ltd* [2018] EWHC 1208 (QB), the approach in *Wilkes* was preferred.

[109a] *Hastings v Finsbury Orthopaedics Ltd* [2022] UKSC 19; 2022 S.L.T. 771 at [15], where the Supreme Court upheld the decision of the first instance judge that the claimant had failed to prove that a prosthetic hip used in total hip replacement surgery was defective.

Producers

Replace footnote 120 with:

16-43 [120] e.g. food processors producing frozen foods from agricultural products; refiners, whose industrial processes in working on extracted minerals produce changes in the essential characteristics and an end-product, such as petroleum spirits from the crude oil won. In *Pearson v Northern Powergrid (Northeast) Plc* unreported 26 April 2022 CC (Middlesbrough), HH Judge Mark Gargan held that it was arguable that the defendant fell within s.1(2)(c) because they produced "domestic electricity" (a species of electricity under the Act) by "carrying out the process which has converted the electricity as generated into low voltage power which can be utilised in a domestic setting."

5. Liability for Defective Digital Content

Where the Consumer Rights Act 2015 does not apply

Replace paragraph 16-166 with:

16-166 Where personal data is required by digital content this should be handled in accordance with the UK General Data Protection Regulation and the Data Protection Act 2018.[402] Where data is not handled in accordance with the requirements of the UK General Data Protection Regulation the data subject may have a claim for damages.[403]

[402] Regulation 2016/679 on the protection of natural persons with regard to the processing of personal data and on the free movement of such data [2016] OJ L119/1 as amended by Data Protection, Privacy and Electronic Communications (Amendments etc) (EU Exit) Regulations 2020 (SI 2020/1586).

[403] See UK GDPR art.82 and Data Protection Act 2018 ss.168 and 169. The intricacies of liability for data breaches are beyond the scope of this work.

Chapter 17

DEATH AND CAUSES OF ACTION

Table of Contents

3. The Survival of a Cause of Action

The Law Reform (Miscellaneous Provisions) Act 1934

Replace footnote 272 with:

[272] This includes applications for further damages under a provisional damages award and variations to periodical payments orders: *Guilfoyle v North Middlesex University Hospital NHS Trust* unreported 4 April 2018 CC (London) per HH Judge Roberts and *Power v Bernard Hastie & Co Ltd* [2022] EWHC 1927 (QB); [2022] P.I.Q.R. Q5, which held that *Guilfoyle* was correctly decided. **17-81**

Supplement to the Ninth Edition brings the main work up to date, including the following significant new cases and developments:

- *Percy v Merriman White* (CA): in contribution proceedings s1(4) of the Contribution Act did not obviate the need to prove negligence by the proposed contributor.
- *Application of Manchester Building Society v Grant Thornton UK LLP* to claim against surveyors (*Charles B Lawrence & Associates v Intercommercial Bank Ltd* (PC)) where the counterfactual was rejected, and to structural engineers in *BDW Trading Ltd v URS Corp Ltd*.
- *Spire Property Development LLP v Withers LLP* (CA): the duty assumed by solicitors in email correspondence after the retainer ended is restricted by what was requested by the client.
- *Ashraf v Lester Dominic Solicitors Ltd*: solicitors acting for a bank owed no duty of care to another party.

McGregor on Damages, Second Cumulative Supplement to the Twenty-First Edition

The Hon Justice Mr James Edelman

978-0-414-10427-3
November 2022
Paperback/Westlaw UK/ProView eBook

The Second Cumulative Supplement to the Twenty-First Edition covers all the latest developments in the law of damages since publication of the Twenty-First Edition in December 2020 and the First Supplement to that edition. These include important decisions on licence fee damages, breaches of undertakings as to damages, scope of damages exclusion clauses, liquidated damages for demurrage, penalty clauses, income tax and equitable compensation or disgorgement of profits, undertakings as to damages, the *Simmonds v Castle* uplift, the extent of recovery of care hire costs as damages for loss of use of a car, provisional damages for personal injury, damages for defamation, additional damages for intellectual property infringements, interest and damages for deceit.